Innsky Air Fryer Oven Cookbook 2020-2021

The Complete Guide of Air Fryer Oven Recipe Book for Anyone Who Want to Enjoy Tasty Effortless Dishes and Upgrade Living

By Chef Jenson Blarden

Contents

Description

Eat healthy and tasty meals with Innsky Air-Fryer Oven!

Do you desire to cook for your family's delight? Then the Innsky Air-Fryer Oven is just what you need. It has a unique method of frying food with a drop of oil that makes all snacks cooked with the appliance healthy and crispy.

The size of the Innsky Air Fryer Oven is a blessing, as it makes it easy to cook anything you desire. Satisfy your cravings with small-sized snacks like chips and fries, main items like pork or beef, and sides like mozzarella sticks and Brussel sprouts.

This Innsky Air-Fryer Oven Cookbook is a comprehensive guide on how to operate the appliance. It contains tips and tricks, delectable recipes, common FAQs, and other basics of the appliance that will turn you into a professional. You will find:

- A Brief Description of the Innsky Air-fryer Oven
- Buttons and Functions of the Innsky Air-fryer Oven
- Advantages of using the Innsky Air-fryer Oven
- Tips and Tricks for grilling with the Innsky Air-fryer Oven
- Cleaning and Maintenance for the Innsky Air-fryer Oven
- Great Meal Preparation Ideas on the Innsky Air-fryer Oven
- Common FAQs associated with the Innsky Air-fryer Oven
- Cooking Time for Various Foods
- Conclusion and a Measurement Conversion Chart
- **juicy recipes perfect for Innsky Air-fryer Oven**

Don't miss out on an opportunity for mouthwatering and healthy meals.

Introduction

Eating healthy and tasty has become easy!

The Innsky Air-Fryer Oven has made it easy to enjoy deep-fried food without having to worry about calories. You get to roast your food, bake, grill, and also stew them with this appliance. The Innsky Air-Fryer Oven does an excellent job of creating delicious and healthy treats for the whole family.

You are about to explore a basic description of Innsky Air-Fryer Oven in Chapter One of this book. Tips and tricks of air frying and brilliant meal preparation ideas in Chapter Two, while Chapter Three has answers to some frequently asked questions and a guide to the cooking time for various meals. After getting to know the appliance, you will find some recipes that will inspire you to cook a healthy and tasty meal for your family.

Enjoy!

Chapter 1: Innsky Air-Fryer Oven 101

What is Innsky Air-Fryer Oven?

The Innsky Air-Fryer Oven is an appliance of great capacity. It is large and, at the same time, sleek and well-built. Its large size makes it fit enough to cook large portions of food in one shot. The Innsky Air-Fryer Oven makes you a real pro, with its LED digital touch screen panel that sets you up for whatever meal you are preparing.

The Innsky Air-Fryer Oven has a 360° hot air circulation technology that gives food a tasty and crisp finishing. It also has a temperature range of 180°F – 400°F and 1700 watts electrical capacity that makes it cook fast and good.

The Innsky Air-Fryer has a detachable cooking basket and pan, which makes it easy to clean and maintain.

Another exciting feature of the Innsky Air-fryer Oven is the auto shut-off and memory function. This makes it start and stop cooking automatically; this way, you don't have to worry about getting your food burnt. The Innsky Air-Fryer Oven is very convenient and great for any lifestyle.

Button and Functions of the Innsky Air-Fryer Oven

The Innsky Air-Fryer Oven has 13 buttons that control every cooking you would be doing with the appliance. Here are the buttons with their functions:

- **LCD Display:** The LCD contains all the other buttons that control the appliance. It is like the motherboard of the Innsky Air Fryer Oven. It shows the cooking time and temperature.
- **Temperature Indicator:** This displays the cooking temperature
- **Working Indicator:** The working indicator keeps flashing throughout the cooking time. It only shows that the food is still cooking.
- **Time Indicator:** This displays the cooking time. While cooking, the cooking time counts down.
- **Temperature +:** This button increases the temperature.
- **Temperature -:** This button decreases the temperature.
- **Mode Indicators:** The mode indicator allows you to choose your desired cooking mode. There are about eight cooking modes, namely French fries, fish, steaks, shrimps, pizza, chicken, baking, and rotisserie. You can also create custom cooking modes to suit your desire.
- **Light Button:** Once the appliance is connected to a power source, you have to press the light button to turn on/off the light.
- **Power Button:** The Power Button turns on the appliance. You just have to tap the button, and then the appliance is powered on with a beep as the entire control panel lights up. To turn off the Innsky Air-Fryer Oven, tap the button again, it will turn off after about 20 seconds once the fan stops working. The Power button can also start the cooking process once you select the cooking mode.
- **Rotating Button:** If you are using the rotisserie shaft or basket, you want to turn on the rotating button to make the cooking even.
- **Preheat Button:** Once the appliance is on, this button can be used to preheat the oven. This way, the oven is ready for your food.

- **Time -:** the time - decreases the cooking time by 1 minute at each tap.
- **Time +:** the time + increases the cooking time by 1 minute at each tap.

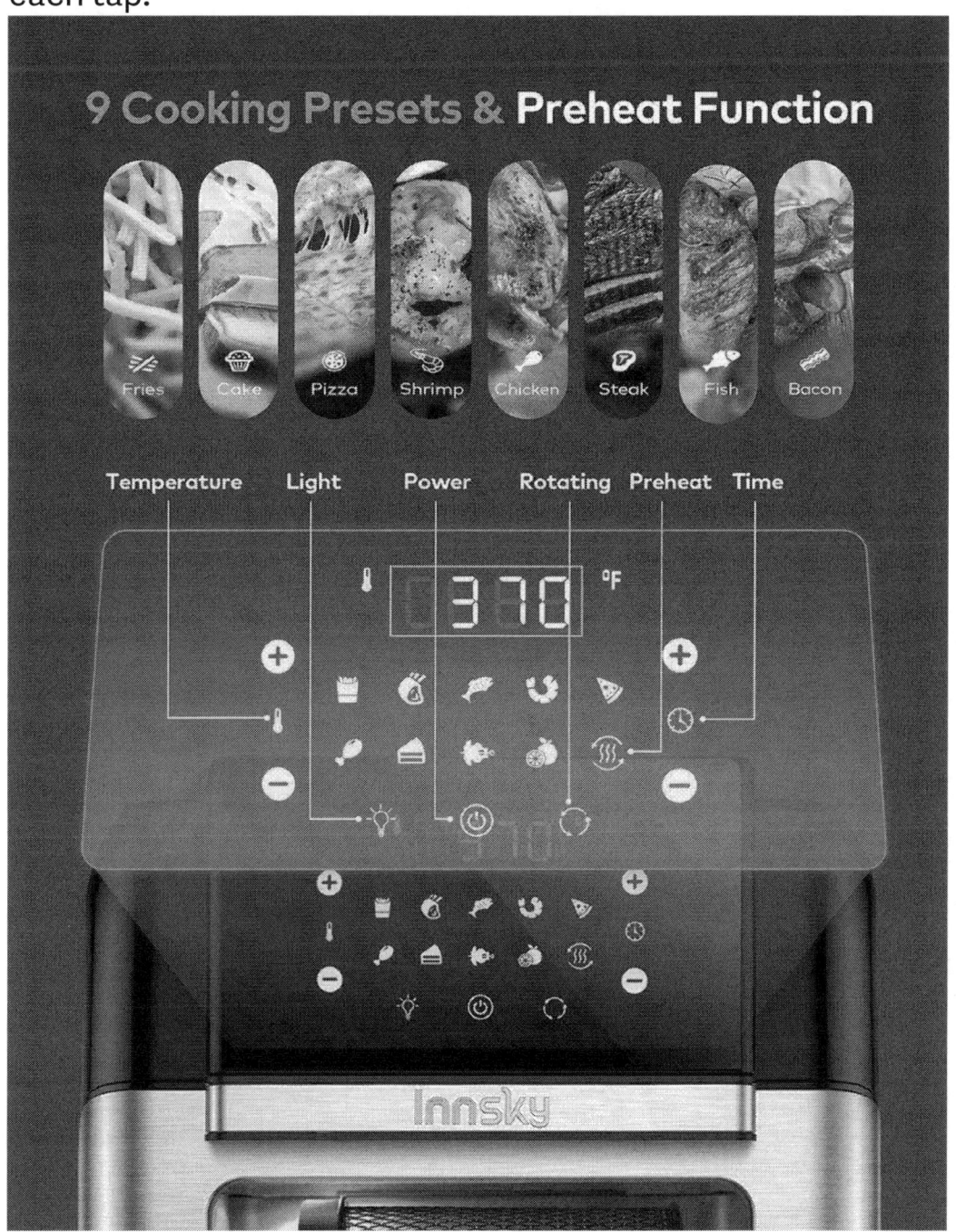

Benefits of using the Innsky Air-Fryer Oven

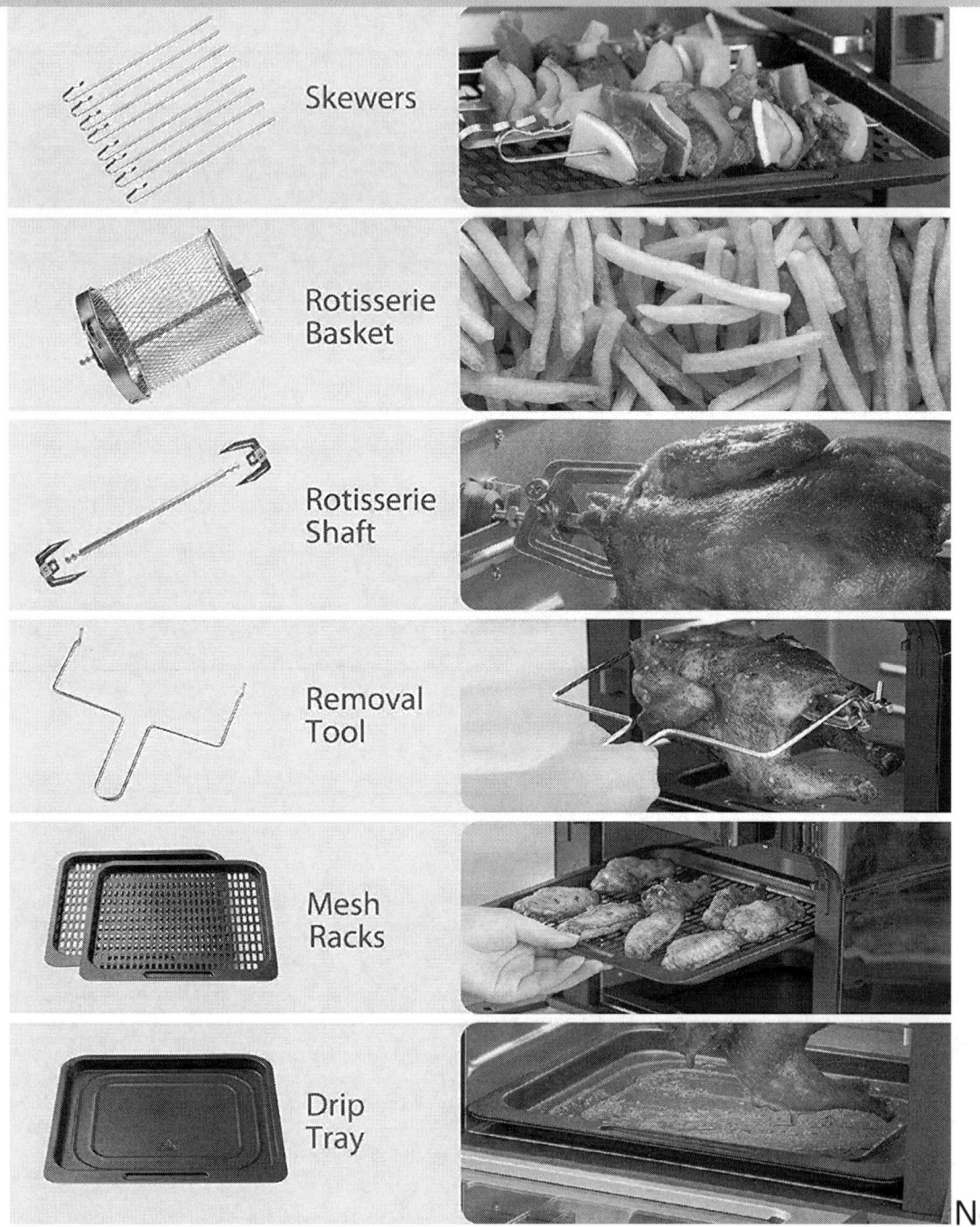

Skewers

Rotisserie Basket

Rotisserie Shaft

Removal Tool

Mesh Racks

Drip Tray

No doubt, all you've ever wanted is to prepare your food fast and easy without the stress that comes with monitoring it. The Innsky Air-

Fryer Oven is your appliance. These are few of the benefits you stand to gain when cooking with the air fryer-oven:

❖ **Cleaning and cooking at ease:** The appliance has a control panel that makes cooking with it effortless. You get to set your cooking preference, time, temperature, and automate the device to stop when the food is ready.
It also has a cooking chamber that is dishwasher safe and easy to clean with a sponge and soap.

❖ **Cook as you desire:** With Innsky Air-Fryer Oven, you get to perform several feats in your kitchen. You can conveniently roast, bake, grill, stew, and fry all on one appliance. It is also great for foods like chicken wings, vegetables, and appetizers like coquettes.

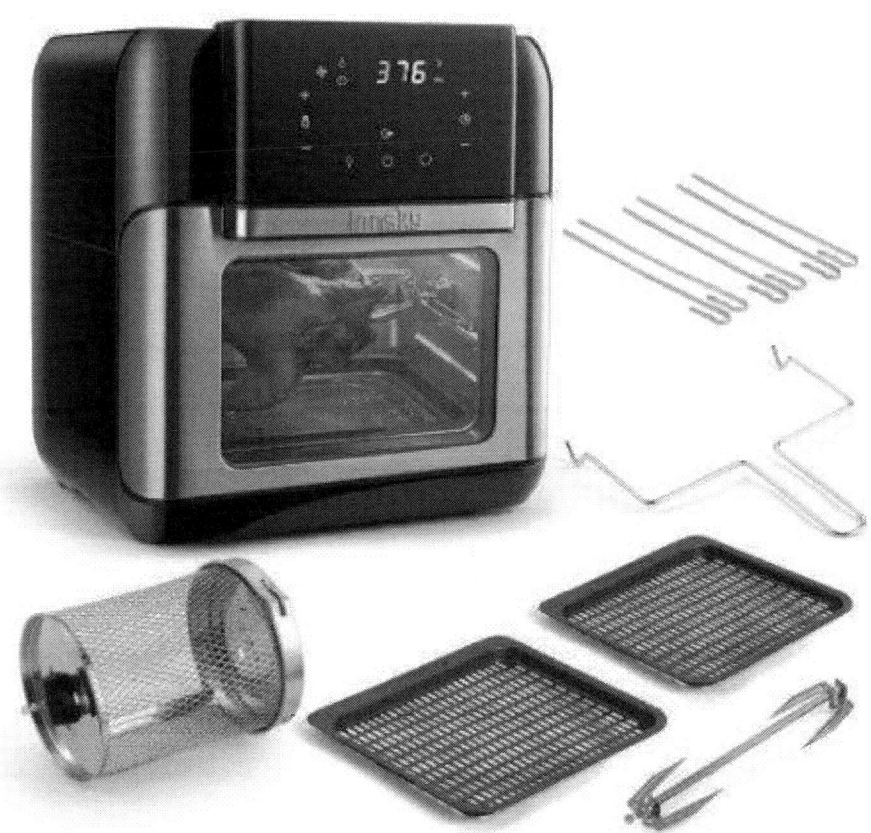

Cleaning and Maintenance of the Innsky Air-Fryer Oven

The Innsky Air-Fryer Oven requires a lot of attention and care. You may want to do the following to ensure maximum care and maintenance:

- ❖ After every use, always clean the air fryer oven, unplug the power cord and be sure the appliance is cool before cleaning.
- ❖ Though the accessories are dishwasher safe, never use hard cleaning materials or utensils to wipe or scratch the surface
- ❖ To ensure easy removal of sticky food, soak the accessories in soapy water
- ❖ Always use warm cloth damped with a mild detergent to wipe the surface
- ❖ Ensure to always remove all unwanted food residue from the control panel with a soft cleaning brush
- ❖ Always store the appliance after cleaning and drying
- ❖ Don't forget to unplug the appliance and let it cool thoroughly before storing in a dry place.

Chapter 2: Tips and Tricks for Successful Grilling with the Innsky Air-fryer Oven

Get ready to be a kitchen God with the tips and tricks you are about to explore. Some of which are:

- **Always check the cooking temperature:** What you want is a nice, well-heated fryer. Hence, you should pay attention to the cooking temperature.
- **Even cooking is the best cooking:** If you are cooking smaller food like fries, wings, ensure to shake the basket at least twice. This way, the food will cook evenly.
- **Overcrowding the basket is undercooking:** Never stock the oven with a lot of items at once. Ensure the basket has just enough items to allow for air to circulate in the oven.
- **Always preheat:** Heating the oven before using it is never a bad idea. Always preheat for at least 3 minutes to give the appliance enough time to reach the temperature you need.
- **Excess smoke is the enemy here:** If you are cooking food with high fat like pork, ensure to empty the fat at the bottom of the oven occasionally. If you notice the food has congealed, pat it dry before cooking to avoid excess oil.
- **Be careful as you bread:** If you have to bread the food, coat in small batches while ensuring that the breading sticks are not too dry.
- **Keep your meat thermometer handy:** The meat may already look brown, but it still needs more heat. Always measure the meat with a thermometer before removing it.

Great Meal Preparation Ideas on the Innsky Air-Fryer Oven

The Innsky Air-Fryer Oven has an excellent way of providing tasty, delectable, and healthy meals without breaking a sweat. It gives your meal a crispy-fried texture; this is because of the super-hot air that makes it cook quickly and evenly.

Just in case you are new to Innsky Air-Fryer oven, or you are running out of meal ideas, here are a few that will change your cooking game:

❖ Juicy Pork Chops

This snack is super juicy and crispy in a delightful way. All you need is a quick shake and bake coating. It is easy to prepare and tasty for everyone.

❖ Air Fryer brownies

Brownies are everyone's favorite. It is a quick 20-22-minute meal with a crispy top that gives this brilliant taste. With this air-fryer oven, you can even cook enough to serve 20 people conveniently.

❖ Air Fryer Brussels Sprouts and Salmon

This meal is one out of a million reasons to love the Air-Fryer Oven. It is a simple recipe that requires only a few minutes to bring delight to the family's table.

❖ Air Fryer Mini Calzones

Are you having a picnic or family dinner? Mini Calzones should be on your menu. It is entertaining and great for any time of the day. All you need is some dough and filling.

❖ Crispy Fried Spring Rolls

Get the most of your appliances with this meal. The crispy fried spring roll is fantastic, especially when it is served with sweet chili sauce or soy sauce.

❖ Air-Fryer Buttermilk Fried Chicken

This should be the number one meal on your menu. It is the exact crispy, juicy snack you've been craving.

Chapter 3: Common FAQs for the Innsky Air-Fryer Oven

Innsky Air-Fryer Oven provides a unique method of cooking. This method may be new to beginners and novice. Hence, here are a few answers to questions you may have as to how the appliance operates:

❖ **The oven's door won't open, what do I do?**

This will only happen when the pressure inside the air-fryer oven is not equal to the one outside the air fryer oven. When this happens, power the air fryer and use the preheat function to heat the inner oven before trying to open again.

❖ **If I have to dehydrate, what is the lowest temperature I can use?**

For dehydrating purposes, the lowest temperature is 90°F.

❖ **I noticed the oven is not cooking evenly on the top and bottom rack. What do I do?**

This appliance is different from the traditional oven, which has a fan built at the rear. The Innsky Air-Fryer Oven has hot airflow from the top of the oven to the bottom. What you do to ensure even cooking is to make sure you do not stack the oven with too much food, as this will only stop air circulation.

❖ **Can I use this appliance to defrost my food?**

Certainly! This appliance is built with a great heating system that can defrost any frozen meat or food.

❖ What is the material of the racks?

The rack and the inside surface of the appliance are made of aluminum alloy. This is what makes the appliance conduct heat properly, which makes it an excellent option for any food you are making.

❖ What is the maximum size of the pan that can fit the appliance?

The inner sizes of the oven are 10.9" long, 9.06" wide, and 6.97" tall. Hence, the appliance can allow pans of 10" x 9" x 0.6".

Cooking Time for Various Foods

Depending on the kind and size of food to be prepared, there are varying cooking times you must consider for optimal results. Here are a few of them:

Food	Amount	Time
Thin frozen fries	1.5-3 cups	15-16 minutes
Homemade fries	1.5-3.5 cups	10-16 minutes
Hash Browns	1 cup	15-18 minutes
Steak	1/4 -1.1 lb	8-12 minutes
Chicken Breast	1/4-1.1 lb	10-15 minutes
Spring Rolls	1/4-3/4 lb	15-20 minutes
Cake	1.25 cups	20-25 minutes
Frozen Onion Rings	1 lb	15 minutes

Sausage Roll	1/4-1.1 lb	13-15 minutes
Pork Chops	1/4-1.1 lb	10-14 minutes
Chicken Drumsticks	1/4-1.1 lb	18-22 minutes
Frozen Chicken Nuggets	1/4-1.1 lb	10-15 minutes
Hamburger	1/4-1.1 lb	7-14 minutes
Muffins	1.25 cups	15-18 minutes
Stuffed vegetables	1/4-1.1 lb	10 minutes

Now, lets head on to the recipes.

Chapter 4: Breakfast and Brunches

Tasty Baked Eggs

Enjoy this easy breakfast recipe that can be prepared with the Innsky Air Fryer Oven. The eggs and the ramekins combine to form a truly nutritious delicacy.

Prep and Cooking Time: 30 minutes | Serves: 4

Ingredients To Use:

- 4 Tbsp of milk
- 1 pound of torn baby spinach
- 4 medium eggs
- 1 Tbsp of olive oil
- Cooking spray
- 7 ounces of chopped ham
- Salt and black pepper, as desired

Step-by-Step Directions to Cook It:

1. Preheat the Innsky Air Fryer Oven to 350°F
2. To a skillet placed over medium heat, add the olive oil, baby spinach, and fry for a few minutes before removing from heat.
3. Coat 4 ramekins with the cooking spray and add equal portions of ham and baby spinach to them.
4. Add an egg, 1 Tbsp of milk, salt, and pepper to each ramekin, then transfer to the preheated Innsky Air Fryer Oven and bake for about 20 minutes.
5. Serve.

Nutritional value per serving:

Calories: 321kcal, Carbs: 15g, Fat: 6g, Protein: 12g

Rustic Breakfast

This basic breakfast recipe is good for days when you have to hurry to work. It can be prepared in a short time and does require active monitoring.

Prep and Cooking Time: 22 minutes | Serves: 4

Ingredients To Use:

- 4 medium eggs
- 7 ounces of baby spinach
- 8 halved tomatoes,
- 4 bacon slices, diced
- 1 garlic clove, thinly sliced
- 4 chipolatas
- 8 halved chestnuts mushrooms
- Salt and black pepper, as desired
- Vegetable oil spray

Step-by-Step Directions to Cook It:

1. Preheat the Innsky Air Fryer Oven to 350°F
2. Spray the vegetable oil on a cooking pan, then add the halved mushrooms, tomatoes, garlic, bacon, spinach, chipolatas, and finally eggs.
3. Season the mixture with salt and pepper, then transfer the cooking pan to the Innsky Air Fryer Oven. Cook for 12 minutes.
4. Divide into equal portions and serve.

Nutritional value per serving:

Calories: 312 kcal, Carbs: 15g, Fat: 6 g, Protein: 5g

Sweet Breakfast Casserole

The Sweet Breakfast Casserole is a highly nutritious meal. The combination of the sugars and the cinnamon powder adds flavor to the recipe. Ensure you try it out on your Innsky Air Fryer Oven.

Prep and Cooking Time: 40 minutes | Serves: 4

Ingredients To Use:

- 1/2 cup of flour
- 4 Tbsp of butter
- 2 Tbsp of white sugar
- 3 Tbsp of brown sugar
- 1/2 tsp of cinnamon powder

Casserole Ingredients

- 1-2/3 cup of blueberries
- 1 tsp baking powder
- 2 cups of buttermilk
- 4 Tbsp butter
- 2 Tbsp white sugar
- 2-1/2 cups of white flour
- 1 lemon, zested and grated
- 4 medium eggs
- 1/2 cup of milk
- 1 tsp baking soda

Step-by-Step Directions to Cook It:

1. Preheat the Innsky Air Fryer Oven to 300°F
2. To a medium bowl, add all the casserole ingredients and mix thoroughly. Transfer the mixture to a cooking pan that fits into the Innsky Air Fryer Oven.

3. In a separate bowl, mix the rest of the ingredients until you obtain a crumble. Add the crumble to the blueberries mix in the Air Fryer Oven cooking pan, then bake for 30 minutes.
4. Divide into equal portions and serve.

Nutritional value per serving:

Calories: 214 kcal, Carbs: 12g, Fat: 5g, Protein: 5g

Polenta Bites

Prepare this delicacy on the mornings you crave for a sugar rush. The bites will leave you energized and ready to start your day.

Prep and Cooking Time: 30 minutes| Serves: 5

Ingredients To Use:

- 3 cups of water
- 1 Tbsp butter
- 1 cup of cornmeal
- Salt and black pepper, as desired

For bites

- 2 Tbsp powdered sugar
- Vegetable oil spray

Step-by-Step Directions to Cook It:

1. Preheat the Innsky Air Fryer Oven to 380°F
2. Mix the water, cornmeal, salt, butter, and pepper in a medium pan, then place over medium heat. Bring to a boil and cook for 8 minutes to make the polenta.
3. Scoop 1 Tbsp of the prepared polenta, use it to form a ball, then place it in a cooking basket. Do this for the rest of the polenta in the cooking pan. Spray the vegetable oil on them and cover.
4. Cook for 10 minutes.
5. Divide the polenta bites into equal portions, sprinkle with powdered sugar, then serve.

Nutritional value per serving:

Calories: 231kcal, Carbs: 12g, Fat: 7g, Protein: 4g

Innsky Air Fried Sandwich

This sandwich is one of the fastest meals you can make with your Innsky Air Fryer Oven. It also fries the eggs without the use of oil, just as promised in chapter 1.

Prep and Cooking Time: 15 minutes| Serves: 2

Ingredients To Use:

- 2 strips of bacon
- 2 medium eggs
- 2 English muffins, halved
- Salt and black pepper, as desired

Step-by-Step Directions to Cook It:

1. Crack the eggs, then add it to the Innsky Air Fryer Oven.
2. Add the bacon strips, cover, and cook at 392°F for 5 minutes.
3. Warm the muffins in a microwave for about 30 seconds, then serve on a plate. Divide the Air Fried eggs on the muffins, add a strip of bacon each, then season with salt and pepper.
4. Cover up the muffins and serve.

Nutritional value per serving:

Calories: 261kcal, Carbs: 12g, Fat: 5g, Protein: 4g

Ham Breakfast Pie

This ham pie recipe is easy to prepare and delicious. Enjoy this delicacy during the weekends when the whole family is available for breakfast.

Prep and Cooking Time: 35 minutes | Serves: 6

Ingredients To Use:

- 2 medium eggs, beaten
- 16 ounces of crescent rolls dough, halved
- 1 Tbsp of grated parmesan
- 2 cups of shredded cheddar cheese
- 2 cups of ham, boiled and sliced
- Salt and black pepper, as desired
- Vegetable oil spray
- Scallions to garnish

Step-by-Step Directions to Cook It:

1. Coat the Innsky Air Fryer Oven's cooking pan with the vegetable oil spray, then press half of the dough on the bottom of the air fryer.
2. To a bowl, add the beaten eggs, cheddar cheese, salt, pepper, and parmesan. Whisk the ingredients thoroughly.
3. Pour the whisked ingredients over the dough in the air fryer.
4. Add the ham over the whisked ingredients, then slice the leftover dough into strips, then add it to the Innsky Air Fryer Oven
5. Bake for 25 minutes at 300°F.
6. Garnish with scallions. Serve.

Nutritional value per serving:

Calories: 400kcal, Carbs: 22g, Fat: 27g, Protein: 16g

Air Fried Tofu Breakfast

With the Innsky Air Fryer Oven, it is possible to fry foods with just a drop of oil. Witness it in this lovely tofu recipe.

Prep and Cooking Time: 22 minutes| Serves: 2

Ingredients To Use:

- 1 tofu block, pressed and cubed
- 1/4 cup of cornstarch
- 1 Tbsp of smoked paprika
- Vegetable oil spray
- Salt and black pepper, as desired

Step-by-Step Directions to Cook It:

1. Coat the Innsky Air Fryer Oven's basket with the oil spray, then preheat the air fryer to 370°F
2. Mix the cubed tofu, paprika, cornstarch, salt, and pepper in a bowl. Stir until well-combined
3. Pour the tofu into the preheated Innsky Air Fryer oven's basket and cook for 12 minutes, stirring the Air Fryer every 4 minutes.
4. Divide into equal portions and serve.

Nutritional value per serving:

Calories: 172kcal, Carbs: 12g, Fat: 4g, Protein: 4g

Potato Frittata

The greatest advantage of the Innsky Air Fryer Oven is the speed at which it prepares food. This lovely frittata meal can be made first thing in the morning, without causing any delay.

Prep and Cooking Time: 30 minutes | Serves: 6

Ingredients To Use:

- 1/2 cup of shredded parmesan
- 12 medium eggs, beaten
- 16 potato wedges
- 6 Tbsp of ricotta cheese
- 2 Tbsp of parsley, chopped
- 3 garlic cloves, grated
- 2 Tbsp chives, chopped
- Salt and black pepper, as desired
- Vegetable oil spray
- 6 ounces of red bell peppers, roasted and chopped

Step-by-Step Directions to Cook It:

1. Mix the eggs, bell peppers, parsley, garlic, ricotta, salt, and pepper in a bowl. Whisk thoroughly.
2. Preheat your Innsky Air Fryer Oven to 300°F and coat it with oil spray.
3. Divide the potato wedges into equal portions, then add the first half to the bottom of the air fryer and sprinkle half of the shredded parmesan on it.
4. Divide the egg mixture into two equal portions, then add the first portion to the air fryer. This will form the first layer of the frittata.

5. Add the rest of the ingredients in the following order, potato wedges, parmesan, then egg mix for the second layer of the frittata.
6. Top the frittata with chives and bake for 20 minutes.
7. Divide into equal portions and serve.

Nutritional value per serving:

Calories: 312kcal, Carbs: 16g, Fat: 6g, Protein: 5g

Blackberry French Toast

This recipe is truly a delight. Within minutes, the Innsky Air Fryer Oven will have the blackberry french toast on your plate.
Prep and Cooking Time: 30 minutes| Serves: 6

Ingredients To Use:

- 1 cup of blackberry jam, warm
- 4 medium eggs
- 8 ounces cream cheese, sliced into cubes
- 1/2 cup of brown sugar
- 1 tsp cinnamon powder
- 2 cups of half and half
- 1 tsp vanilla extract
- 12 ounces of bread loaf, sliced into cubes
- Vegetable oil spray.

Step-by-Step Directions to Cook It:

1. Coat your Innsky Air Fryer Oven with oil spray, then preheat it to 300°F
2. Add the blackberry jam to the bottom of the air fryer, layer it with half of the cubed bread, then add the cubed cheese and top with the remainder of the bread cubes.
3. To a bowl, add the eggs, half and half, sugar, cinnamon, and vanilla. Whisk thoroughly, then add to the bread mix in the Innsky Air Fryer.
4. Toast for 20 minutes, then divide into equal portions and serve.

Nutritional value per serving:

Calories: 215kcal, Carbs: 16g, Fat: 6g, Protein: 6g

Tasty Hash

The result of this Hash recipe in the Innsky Air Fryer Oven is marvelous. It can be prepared in just a few steps.
Prep and Cooking Time: 25 minutes | Serves: 6

Ingredients To Use:

- 1/2 tsp paprika
- 1 egg, beaten
- 1/4 cup of olive oil
- 2 Tbsp chives, chopped
- 16 ounces of hash browns
- 1/2 tsp garlic powder
- 1 cup of shredded cheddar
- Salt and black pepper, as desired

Step-by-Step Directions to Cook It:

1. Add the olive oil to the Innsky Air Fryer Oven, then preheat it to 350°F.
2. Add the hash browns, paprika, egg, garlic, salt, and pepper. Mix until well combined in the air fryer.
3. Cook for 14 minutes.
4. Top the hash with the chives and shredded cheddar.
5. Divide into equal portions and serve.

Nutritional value per serving:

Calories: 213kcal, Carbs: 12g, Fat: 7g, Protein: 4g

Chapter 5: Red Meat Recipes

Seasoned Rib Eye Steak

This recipe involves frying a whole Ribeye steak with just a tablespoon of oil. This can only be possible with the Innsky Air Fryer Oven.

Prep and Cooking Time: 30 minutes | Serves: 4

Ingredients To Use:

- 2 pounds of ribeye steak
- 1 Tbsp olive oil
- Salt and black pepper, as desired

Rub Ingredients

- 1 Tbsp cumin, ground
- 1 Tbsp rosemary, dried
- 2 Tbsp onion powder
- 1 Tbsp brown sugar
- 2 Tbsp oregano, dried
- 3 Tbsp sweet paprika
- 2 Tbsp garlic powder

Step-by-Step Directions to Cook It:

1. Set the Innsky Air Fryer Oven to Steak Mode and preheat to 400°F
2. Mix the onions, garlic, sugar, rosemary, oregano, salt, cumin, and pepper in a bowl to prepare the rub.

3. Coat the rub on the steak, then season again with pepper and salt. Brush the steak with the olive oil, then transfer it to Innsky Air Fryer Oven.
4. Cook for 20 minutes, flipping after 10 minutes.
5. Remove the steak and carve on a chopping board.
6. Serve with salad.

Nutritional value per serving:

Calories: 320kcal, Carbs: 22g, Fat: 8g, Protein: 21 58.4g

Chinese Steak and Broccoli

The combination of oyster sauce, soy sauce, and sesame oil in this recipe add a burst of flavor to the steak.

Prep and Cooking Time: 50 minutes | Serves: 4

Ingredients To Use:

- 3/4 pound of round steak, stripped
- 1 garlic clove, grated
- 1 tsp soy sauce
- 1 pound of broccoli florets
- 1 tsp sugar
- 1/3 cup of sherry
- 1 Tbsp olive oil
- 2 tsp sesame oil
- 1/3 cup of oyster sauce
- A handful of parsley to garnish

Step-by-Step Directions to Cook It:

1. Set the Innsky Air Fryer Oven to Steak Mode and preheat to 380°F
2. Mix the oyster sauce, sesame oil, sugar, sherry, soy sauce, and beef in a bowl. Mix until the meat is well-coated. Set aside for 25 minutes.
3. Prepare a cooking pan that fits the Innsky Air Fryer Oven, then add the broccoli, oil, garlic, and beef to the pan.
4. Transfer the pan to the Air fryer and cook for 12 minutes.
5. Divide into equal portions, garnish with parsley, and serve.

Nutritional value per serving:

Calories: 330 kcal, Carbs: 23g, Fat: 7g, Protein: 23g

Beef Fillets with Garlic Mayonnaise

For extra flavor, the beef in this recipe is cooked twice before serving to plates. It tastes incredibly delicious when served with mayonnaise.

Prep and Cooking Time: 50 minutes| Serves: 5

Ingredients To Use:

- 3 pounds of beef fillet
- 1 cup of mayonnaise
- 2 Tbsp chives, chopped
- 1/3 cup of sour cream
- 4 Tbsp mustard
- 1/4 cup of tarragon, chopped
- 2 garlic cloves, grated
- Salt and black pepper, as desired

Step-by-Step Directions to Cook It:

1. Set the Innsky Air Fryer Oven to Steak Mode and preheat to 370°F
2. Season the beef with salt and black pepper as desired, then transfer to the preheated air fryer. Cook at the same temperature for 20 minutes, then remove and set aside.
3. Mix the garlic, sour cream, mayonnaise, chives, salt, and pepper in a bowl. Whisk thoroughly.
4. In a separate bowl, whisk the mustard and tarragon, then add the prepared beef and return to the air fryer. Lower the temperature of the Innsky Air Fryer Oven to 350°F, then cook for another 20 minutes.
5. Divide the beef into equal portions and serve with the garlic mayo as a sauce.

Nutritional value per serving:

Calories: 400kcal, Carbs: 27g, Fat: 12g, Protein: 19g

Pork with Couscous

When eaten alone, the couscous isn't so tasty, but when combined with seasoned pork, it becomes fantastic. You must try it out.

Prep and Cooking Time: 50 minutes | Serves: 5

Ingredients To Use:

- 2 cups couscous, cooked
- 2-1/2 pounds of pork loin, trimmed and boneless
- 1/2 Tbsp sweet paprika
- 1 tsp oregano, dried
- 2-1/4 tsp sage, dried
- 1/2 Tbsp garlic powder
- 1 tsp basil, dried
- 3/4 cup of chicken stock
- 1/4 tsp rosemary, dried
- 2 Tbsp olive oil
- 1/4 tsp marjoram, dried
- Salt and black pepper, as desired

Step-by-Step Directions to Cook It:

1. Set the Innsky Air Fryer Oven to Steak Mode and preheat to 370°F
2. Mix the oil, stock, garlic, paprika, rosemary, oregano, marjoram, salt, pepper, thyme, and sage in a bowl. Mix until well-combined.
3. In a separate bowl, mix the pork and the stock mixture. Leave to marinate for an hour.
4. Transfer the beef and the marinade to a cooking pan that fits the Innsky Air Fryer Oven. Cook for 35 minutes.
5. Divide into equal portions, then serve with couscous.

Nutritional value per serving:

Calories: 310kcal, Carbs: 37g, Fat: 4g, Protein: 34g

Lemony Lamb Leg

The lemon juice added to this recipe brings out the flavor of the lamb. You will experience a pleasant aftertaste when eating the lamb.

Prep and Cooking Time: 1 hour 10 minutes| Serves: 6

Ingredients To Use:

- 4 pounds of lamb leg
- 2 Tbsp parsley, chopped
- 2 pounds of baby potatoes
- 2 Tbsp olive oil
- 3 garlic cloves, grated
- 2 Tbsp lemon juice
- 1 Tbsp lemon rind, grated
- 1 cup of beef stock
- 2 springs rosemary, chopped
- 2 Tbsp oregano, chopped
- Salt and black pepper, as desired

Step-by-Step Directions to Cook It:

1. Coat the Innsky Air Fryer Oven with 1 Tbsp of olive oil, then preheat it to 360°F
2. With a small knife, make cuts all over the lamb leg. Insert chopped rosemary springs, then season with salt and black pepper.
3. In a bowl, mix the oregano, 1 Tbsp of oil, garlic, lemon juice, parsley, and rind. Coat the lamb leg with the mixture.
4. Transfer the baby potatoes to a cooking pan that fits the air fryer and then cook for 3 minutes.
5. Add the lamb and stock mix to the air fryer, then cook for 1 hour.
6. Divide into equal portions and serve.

Nutritional value per serving:

Calories: 264kcal, Carbs: 27g, Fat: 4g, Protein: 32g

Beef Curry

When cooking this meal, beware of your neighbors. The aroma of this meal is sure to attract all and sundry.

Prep and Cooking Time: 1 hour | Serves: 4

Ingredients To Use:

- 2 pounds of beef steak, cubed
- 10 ounces of canned coconut milk
- 3 potatoes, diced
- 1 Tbsp wine mustard
- 2 Tbsp tomato sauce
- 2-1/2 Tbsp curry powder
- 2 garlic cloves, grated
- 2 yellow onions, chopped
- 2 Tbsp olive oil
- Salt and black pepper, as desired

Step-by-Step Directions to Cook It:

1. Set the Innsky Air Fryer Oven to Steak Mode and preheat to 350°F
2. Sauté the garlic and onions with the 2 Tbsp of olive oil in a cooking pan that fits your Innsky Air Fryer Oven.
3. Add mustard and potatoes, stir, then cook for another minute.
4. Add the beef, curry, salt, coconut milk, pepper, and tomato. Transfer the pan to the Innsky Air Fryer and cook for 40 minutes.
5. Divide into equal portions and serve.

Nutritional value per serving:

Calories: 432kcal, Carbs: 20g, Fat: 16g, Protein: 27g

Stuffed Pork Steaks

The juicy taste of the meat is combined with the vegetables and cheese stuffed in-between. You get the feeling of a burger without the bread.

Prep and Cooking Time: 30 minutes| Serves: 4

Ingredients To Use:

- 2 limes, zested and grated
- Juice from 2 limes
- 4 pork loin steaks
- 1 orange, zested and grated
- Juice from 1 orange
- 1 cup of mint, chopped
- 4 tsp garlic, grated
- 1 cup of cilantro, chopped
- 1 tsp oregano, dried
- 2 tsp cumin, ground
- 3/4 cup of olive oil
- 4 ham slices
- 2 Tbsp mustard
- 2 pickles, chopped
- 6 Swiss cheese slices
- Salt and black pepper, as desired

Step-by-Step Directions to Cook It:

1. Set the Innsky Air Fryer Oven to Steak Mode and preheat to 340°F
2. Add the lime and orange zest, lime and orange juice, oil, garlic, oregano, cilantro, black pepper, salt, cumin, and mint to a food

processor. Pulse until a smooth texture is obtained.
3. In a bowl, season pork steaks with salt and black pepper, then add the marinade and toss.
4. Put the steaks on a chopping board or flat surface, divide equal portions of ham, mustard, pickles, and cheese on them, then roll and spear with toothpicks.
5. Transfer stuffed steaks to the Innsky Air Fryer Oven and cook for 20 minutes.
6. Divide into equal portions and serve with salad.

Nutritional value per serving:

Calories: 270kcal, Carbs: 13g, Fat: 7g, Protein: 20g

Tasty Lamb Ribs

This recipe replicates the taste of deep-fried flour chicken. The flour bakes around the lamb and gives it a fantastic taste.

Prep and Cooking Time: 1 hour| Serves: 8

Ingredients To Use:

- 8 lamb ribs
- 2 carrots, chopped
- 3 Tbsp white flour
- 2 Tbsp extra virgin olive oil
- 2 cups of veggie stock
- 4 garlic cloves, grated
- 1 Tbsp rosemary, chopped
- Salt and black pepper, as desired

Step-by-Step Directions to Cook It:

1. Set the Innsky Air Fryer Oven to Steak Mode and preheat to 360°F
2. Season the lamb ribs with salt and black pepper, brush with oil and minced garlic, then transfer to the air fryer.
3. Cook at the same temperature for 10 minutes.
4. In a heatproof dish, mix the flour and stock. Add the lamb ribs, rosemary, and carrots, and then transfer to the Innsky Air Fryer. Reduce the temperature and cook at 350°F for 30 minutes.
5. Divide into equal portions and serve immediately.

Nutritional value per serving:

Calories: 302kcal, Carbs: 22g, Fat: 7g, Protein: 27g

Mexican Beef Mix

The sauce tastes just right with the beef roast used. Try this recipe out on your Innsky Air Fryer Oven when you're feeling adventurous.

Prep and Cooking Time: 1 hour 30 minutes | Serves: 8

Ingredients To Use:

- 2 pounds of beef roast, diced
- 1/2 cup of water
- 2 Tbsp olive oil
- 2 green bell peppers, chopped
- 4 jalapenos, chopped
- 2 yellow onions, chopped
- 1 habanero pepper, chopped
- 14 ounces canned tomatoes, chopped
- 6 garlic cloves, grated
- 1 and 1/2 tsp cumin, ground
- 2 Tbsp cilantro, chopped
- 1 tsp oregano, dried
- Salt and black pepper, as desired

Step-by-Step Directions to Cook It:

1. Set the Innsky Air Fryer Oven to Steak Mode and preheat to 300°F
2. Mix the beef, oil, bell peppers, jalapenos, onions, tomatoes, habanero, garlic, cumin, oregano, cilantro, salt, pepper, and water in a cooking pan. Ensure the pan fits your Innsky Air Fryer Oven.
3. Transfer the pan to the air fryer and cook for 1 hour 10 minutes.
4. Divide into equal portions and serve.

Nutritional value per serving:

Calories: 63kcal, Carbs: 37.4g, Fat: 60.6g, Protein: 58.4g

Air Fried Pork Shoulder

Taste the difference with this recipe prepared on the Innsky Air Fryer Oven. The pork shoulder is well prepared and tastes better than any other.

Prep and Cooking Time: 2 hours | Serves: 6

Ingredients To Use:

- 3 Tbsp of minced garlic
- 4 pounds of pork shoulder
- 3 Tbsp olive oil
- Salt and black pepper, as desired

Step-by-Step Directions to Cook It:

1. Set the Innsky Air Fryer Oven to Steak Mode and preheat to 390°F
2. Mix the olive oil, salt, and black pepper in a bowl. Whisk and brush it over the pork shoulders.
3. Transfer to the preheated air fryer and cook for 10 minutes
4. Reduce the temperature of the Innsky Air Fryer to 300°F by pressing the *Temperature* – button on the LCD. Cook at this temperature for 1 hour 10 minutes.
5. Carve the pork shoulder and serve with salad.

Nutritional value per serving:

Calories: 221 kcal, Carbs: 7g, Fat: 4g, Protein: 10g

Chapter 6: Poultry Recipes

Easy Chicken Thighs and Baby Potatoes

The potatoes are infused with flavor by cooking it alongside the chicken. It melts in the mouth and combines well with the chicken.

Prep and Cooking Time: 40 minutes | Serves: 4

Ingredients To Use

- 8 drumsticks
- 2 tsp oregano, dried
- 1 pound of baby potatoes, cut into halves
- 2 tsp thyme, chopped
- 2 tsp rosemary, dried
- 1 red onion, chopped
- 1/2 tsp sweet paprika
- 2 Tbsp olive oil
- 2 garlic cloves, grated
- Salt and black pepper, as desired

Step-by-Step Directions to Cook It:

1. Set the Innsky Air Fryer Oven to Chicken Mode and preheat to 400°F
2. Mix the drumsticks, potatoes, salt, black pepper, paprika, thyme, rosemary, onion, oregano, garlic, and oil in a bowl.
3. Coat the chicken thoroughly, then transfer to a heatproof dish that fits Innsky Air Fryer Oven and cook for 30 minutes. Shake after 15 minutes.
4. Divide into equal portions and serve

Nutritional value per serving:

Calories: 364kcal, Carbs: 21g, Fat: 14g, Protein: 34g

Chicken and Capers

This is a beautiful recipe for a Saturday night relaxation. The chicken will goes really well with capers and beer.

Prep and Cooking Time: 30 minutes | Serves: 5

Ingredients To Use:

- 4 drumsticks
- 1/2 cup of chicken stock
- 4 garlic cloves, grated
- 1 lemon, sliced
- 3 Tbsp capers
- 3 Tbsp butter, melted
- 4 green onions, chopped
- Salt and black pepper, as desired

Step-by-Step Directions to Cook It:

1. Set the Innsky Air Fryer Oven to Chicken Mode and preheat to 370°F
2. Rub the chicken with the butter, salt, and pepper, then place the coated chicken in a baking dish that fits your air fryer.
3. Add the garlic, capers, lemon slices, and chicken stock to the baking dish. Toss until well-combined, then move the baking dish to the air fryer oven.
4. Cook for 20 minutes, shaking after 10 minutes.
5. Garnish with green onions, divide into equal portions and serve.

Nutritional value per serving:

Calories: 200kcal, Carbs: 17g, Fat: 9g, Protein: 7g

Honey Duck Breasts

Honey automatically makes everything taste better. It contributes to this recipe by enhancing the flavor and aroma of the chicken and spices.

Prep and Cooking Time: 32 minutes| Serves: 2

Ingredients To Use:

- 1 smoked duck breast, halved
- 1/2 tsp apple vinegar
- 1 tsp honey
- 1 Tbsp mustard
- 1 tsp tomato paste

Step-by-Step Directions to Cook It:

1. Set the Innsky Air Fryer Oven to Chicken Mode and preheat to 370°F
2. Mix the honey, tomato paste, vinegar, mustard, and duck breasts in a medium bowl. Toss until well-combined.
3. Transfer the coated duck breast to the preheated Innsky Air Fryer Oven and cook for 15 minutes.
4. Remove the duck breast from the air fryer, coat with honey, then return to the air fryer and cook at the same temperature for another 6 minutes.
5. Divide into equal portions and serve.

Nutritional value per serving:

Calories: 274kcal, Carbs: 22g, Fat: 11g, Protein: 13g

Mexican Chicken

Recreate the Mexican food stall experience with this delicious chicken salsa meal.

Prep and Cooking Time: 30 minutes| Serves: 4

Ingredients To Use:

- 16 ounces Salsa Verde
- 1/4 cup of cilantro, chopped
- 1-1/2 cup of grated Monterey Jack cheese
- 1 pound of chicken breast, deboned and skinned
- 1 Tbsp olive oil
- 1 tsp garlic powder
- Salt and black pepper, as desired

Step-by-Step Directions to Cook It:

1. Set the Innsky Air Fryer Oven to Chicken Mode and preheat to 380°F
2. Add the salsa Verde to a baking dish that fits the Innsky Air Fryer Oven.
3. Season the chicken breast with salt, black pepper, garlic, and olive oil, and then place the seasoned chicken over the salsa Verde.
4. Transfer the baking dish to the air fryer oven and cook for 20 minutes.
5. Sprinkle cheese over the top and cook for another 2 minutes.
6. Divide into equal portions and serve.

Nutritional value per serving:

Calories: 340 kcal, Carbs: 32g, Fat: 18g, Protein: 18g

Chicken and Asparagus

Asparagus is a cruciferous vegetable that is rich in nutrients and vitamins. Add steamed asparagus to your air fried chicken t0 start eating healthy and delicious.

Prep and Cooking Time: 30 minutes | Serves: 4

Ingredients To Use:

- 8 chicken wings, halved
- 1 tsp cumin, ground
- 1 Tbsp rosemary, chopped
- 8 asparagus spears
- Salt and black pepper, as desired

Step-by-Step Directions to Cook It:

1. Set the Innsky Air Fryer Oven to Chicken Mode and preheat to 360°F
2. Season the chicken wings with salt, black pepper, rosemary, and cumin.
3. Transfer the coated wings to the Innsky Air Fryer's basket and cook for 20 minutes.
4. To a pan placed over medium heat, add the asparagus and water. Steam for 3 minutes, and then transfer the asparagus to a bowl containing ice water.
5. Drain the asparagus, then divide it into four portions. Add the chicken portions to the asparagus.
6. Serve.

Nutritional value per serving:

Calories: 270kcal, Carbs: 24g, Fat: 8g, Protein: 22g

Chicken Cacciatore

This fried chicken sauce recipe can be prepared in a few minutes. The steps are easy, and the result is lovely.

Prep and Cooking Time: 30 minutes | Serves: 5

Ingredients To Use:

- 8 chicken breasts
- 1/2 cup of black olives, pitted and sliced
- 1 bay leaf
- 1 yellow onion, chopped
- 1 tsp garlic powder
- 28 ounces canned tomatoes and juice, crushed
- 1 tsp oregano, dried
- Salt and black pepper, as desired

Step-by-Step Directions to Cook It:

1. Set the Innsky Air Fryer Oven to Chicken Mode and preheat to 365°F
2. In a heatproof baking dish, mix the chicken, salt, black pepper, bay leaf, garlic, tomatoes, juice, olives, oregano, and onion. Toss until well-combined.
3. Transfer to the preheated air fryer and cook for 20 minutes.
4. Divide into equal portions and serve.

Nutritional value per serving:

Calories: 300kcal, Carbs: 20g, Fat: 12g, Protein: 24g

Lemon Chicken

Lemon is usually synonymous with fried and grilled foods because of its ability to ease their digestion. Try out this recipe and discover a beautiful combination

Prep and Cooking Time: 40 minutes| Serves: 6

Ingredients To Use:

- 1 whole chicken, divided into medium portions
- Juice from 2 lemons
- 1 Tbsp olive oil
- 2 lemons, zested and grated
- Salt and black pepper, as desired

Step-by-Step Directions to Cook It:

1. Set the Innsky Air Fryer Oven to Chicken Mode and preheat to 350°F
2. Season the chicken with salt, pepper, lemon juice, and zest. Also, rub with olive oil.
3. Transfer to the preheated air fryer and cook for 15 per side.
4. Divide the chicken into six portions and serve with salad.

Nutritional value per serving:

Calories: 334kcal, Carbs: 26g, Fat: 24g, Protein: 20g

Chicken and Black Olive Sauce

This chicken recipe doesn't only taste delicious; it is also healthy. The entire chicken breast is fried with just two tablespoons of oil.

Prep and Cooking Time: 18 minutes | Serves: 2

Ingredients To Use:

- 1 chicken breast, quartered
- 3 garlic cloves, grated
- 2 Tbsp olive oil

Sauce Ingredients

- 1 Tbsp lemon juice
- 2 Tbsp olive oil
- 1 cup of black olives, pitted
- 1/4 cup of parsley, chopped
- Salt and black pepper, as desired

Step-by-Step Directions to Cook It:

1. Set the Innsky Air Fryer Oven to Chicken Mode and preheat to 370°F
2. Add the olives, a pinch of salt, black pepper, 2 Tbsp olive oil, parsley, and lemon juice to a food processor. Pulse until a smooth mixture is obtained.
3. Season the four pieces of chicken with salt and black pepper, brush with oil and garlic, then transfer to the preheated air fryer and cook for 8 minutes.
4. Divide the chicken into two servings and top with the prepared olive sauce.
5. Serve.

Nutritional value per serving:

Calories: 270kcal, Carbs: 23g, Fat: 12g, Protein: 22g

Chicken Thighs and Apple Mix

The chicken in this recipe is marinated for 12 hours to ensure the maximum combination of flavor. Experience an explosion of taste in your mouth with this chicken meal.

Prep and Cooking Time: 12 hours 30 minutes | Serves: 4

Ingredients To Use:

- 8 drumsticks
- 1 Tbsp of apple cider vinegar
- 3 apples, cored and quartered
- 3/4 cup of apple juice
- 1/2 cup of maple syrup
- 3 Tbsp onion, sliced
- 1 Tbsp of minced ginger
- 1/2 tsp of dried thyme
- 2 Tbsp of parsley
- Salt and black pepper, as desired

Step-by-Step Directions to Cook It:

1. Set the Innsky Air Fryer Oven to Chicken Mode and preheat to 350°F
2. Mix the drumsticks, salt, pepper, parsley, vinegar, syrup, apple juice, onions, ginger, and thyme. Toss and keep in the refrigerator for 12 hours.
3. After the 12 hours, transfer the chicken and marinade to the preheated Air Fryer and cook for 30 minutes.
4. Divide into equal portions and serve immediately.

Nutritional value per serving:

Calories: 314kcal, Carbs: 34g, Fat: 8g, Protein: 22g

Pepperoni Chicken

This recipe is for lovers of pepperoni and chicken. The chicken here is layered with pepperoni and topped with mozzarella cheese for an extra flavor.

Prep and Cooking Time: 32 minutes | Serves: 6

Ingredients To Use:

- 2 ounces of sliced pepperoni
- 14 ounces of tomato paste
- 1 Tbsp olive oil
- 6 ounces of sliced mozzarella
- 4 medium chicken breasts, skinned and deboned
- 1 tsp of dried oregano, dried
- 1 tsp of garlic powder
- Salt and black pepper, as desired

Step-by-Step Directions to Cook It:

1. Set the Innsky Air Fryer Oven to Rotisserie Mode and preheat to 350°F
2. Mix the chicken breast, salt, pepper, oregano, and garlic in a bowl.
3. Transfer the coated chicken to a cooking pan that fits the preheated air fryer and cook for 6 minutes.
4. Top with mozzarella slices and pepperoni slices, spread tomato paste over chicken and cook for an additional 15 minutes at the same temperature.
5. Divide into equal portions and serve.

Nutritional value per serving:

Calories: 320 kcal, Carbs: 23g, Fat: 10g, Protein: 27g

Chapter 7: Seafood Recipes

Tasty Pollock

The Innsky Air Fryer Oven will have your pollock crispy and ready for you in less than 15 minutes. The butter replaces the oil normally used for frying.

Prep and Cooking Time: 25 minutes | Serves: 6

Ingredients To Use:

- 1/2 cup of sour cream
- 2 Tbsp of melted butter
- 4 boneless Pollock fillets
- Salt and black pepper, as desired
- 1/4 cup of grated parmesan
- Cooking spray

Step-by-Step Directions to Cook It:

1. Set the Innsky Air Fryer Oven to Fish Mode and preheat to 320°F
2. Mix the butter, sour cream, salt, black pepper, and parmesan in a bowl. Whisk until well-combined.
3. Spray the cooking spray on the pollock fillets, then season with salt and black pepper.
4. Coat the sour cream mix on each side of the fillets, then transfer them to the preheated air-fryer—Cook for 15 minutes.
5. Remove from air fryer and serve with salad.

Nutritional value per serving:

Calories: 300kcal, Carbs: 14g, Fat: 13g, Protein: 44g

Air Fried Catfish

Catfish is soft and flaky when fried. Try out this recipe and eat the fish with a spicy sauce for an incredible taste.

Prep and Cooking Time: 20 minutes | Serves: 4

Ingredients To Use:

- 4 catfish fillets
- Sweet paprika, a pinch
- 1 Tbsp lemon juice
- 1 Tbsp of chopped parsley
- 1 Tbsp olive oil
- Salt and black pepper, as desired

Step-by-Step Directions to Cook It:

1. Set the Innsky Air Fryer Oven to Fish Mode and preheat to 350°F
2. Season the catfish with paprika, salt, black pepper, and drizzle with oil.
3. Transfer the seasoned fish to the Innsky Air Fryer Oven's basket and cook for 20 minutes. Flip to the other side after 10 minutes.
4. Divide the catfish fillets into equal portions, sprinkle chopped parsley over the top, and drizzle with lemon juice.
5. Serve.

Nutritional value per serving:

Calories: 253kcal, Carbs: 26g, Fat: 6g, Protein: 22g

Lemony Saba Fish

On its own, Saba fish is delicious. But with lemon and garlic, the combined taste is beyond amazing. The lemon enhances everything.

Prep and Cooking Time: 18 minutes | Serves: 1

Ingredients To Use:

- 4 boneless Saba fish fillets
- 2 Tbsp olive oil
- 2 Tbsp lemon juice
- 2 Tbsp of minced garlic
- 3 red chili pepper, chopped
- Salt and black pepper, as desired

Step-by-Step Directions to Cook It:

1. Set the Innsky Air Fryer Oven to Fish Mode and preheat to 360°F
2. Pour the Saba fish into a bowl and add the salt, black pepper, chili, lemon juice, garlic, and oil. Toss until the fish fillets are well-coated.
3. Transfer to the preheated Air Fryer Oven and cook for 8 minutes. Flip to the other side after 4 minutes.
4. Divide into equal portions and serve with fries (if available)

Nutritional value per serving:

Calories: 300kcal, Carbs: 15g, Fat: 4g, Protein: 15g

Buttered Shrimp Skewers

When you try out this recipe on your Innsky Air Fryer Oven, you will never cook shrimp anywhere else. Try this recipe to find out why.

Prep and Cooking Time: 16 minutes| Serves: 2

Ingredients To Use:

- 8 shrimps, peeled and deveined
- 2 green bell pepper, sliced
- 1 Tbsp rosemary, chopped
- 4 garlic cloves, grated
- 1 Tbsp butter, melted
- Salt and black pepper, as desired

Step-by-Step Directions to Cook It:

1. Set the Innsky Air Fryer Oven to Fish Mode and preheat to 360°F
2. Mix the shrimps, garlic, salt, black pepper, butter, rosemary, and chopped bell pepper in a bowl. Toss until well-combined and then leave to marinate.
3. Arrange the shrimps and bell pepper slices alternatively on a skewer. Each skewer should have 2 shrimps and 2 bell pepper slices. Repeat the process until all the shrimps are arranged on skewers.
4. Transfer the skewers to the preheated Air Fryer Oven's basket and cook for 6 minutes.
5. Divide the skewers into 2 portions and serve hot.

Nutritional value per serving:

Calories: 140kcal, Carbs: 15g, Fat: 1g, Protein: 7g

Shrimp and Crab Mix

This is another shrimp delicacy that you can try with the Innsky Air Fryer Oven. The crabmeat and the flavored shrimp will leave you hungry for more. Luckily the meal can be prepared within 30 minutes.

Prep and Cooking Time: 35 minutes| Serves: 4

Ingredients To Use:

- 1 pound of shrimps, peeled and deveined
- 1/2 cup of sliced yellow onion
- 1 cup of flaked crabmeat
- 1 cup of mayonnaise
- 1 tsp sweet paprika
- 2 Tbsp breadcrumbs
- 1 tsp Worcestershire sauce
- 1 cup of sliced green bell pepper
- 1 Tbsp of melted butter
- Salt and black pepper, as desired

Step-by-Step Directions to Cook It:

1. Set the Innsky Air Fryer Oven to Shrimp Mode and preheat to 320°F
2. Mix the shrimps, crab meat, onions, bell pepper, mayonnaise, salt, black pepper, Worcestershire sauce, and celery in a bowl. Toss well.
3. Transfer the coated shrimps and crab meat to a cooking pan that fits into the Innsky Air Fryer Oven.
4. Sprinkle the paprika and bread crumbs over the shrimp crab mixture, then add melted butter, and place into the preheated

air fryer.

5. Cook for 25 minutes, flipping after 15 minutes.
6. Divide into equal portions and serve.

Nutritional value per serving:

Calories: 200kcal, Carbs: 17g, Fat: 13g, Protein: 19g

Trout Fillet and Orange Sauce

Orange adds a tropical taste to the fish fillet. A bite of the fish coated with orange sauce will totally reeducate you on the importance of cooking with citrus fruits.

Prep and Cooking Time: 20 minutes | Serves: 4

Ingredients To Use:

- 4 trout fillets, skinned and deboned
- 1 Tbsp olive oil
- 4 spring onions, thinly sliced
- 1 Tbsp of grated ginger
- 1 orange, zested and juiced
- Salt and black pepper, as desired

Step-by-Step Directions to Cook It:

1. Set the Innsky Air Fryer Oven to Fish Mode and preheat to 360°F
2. Season the trout with salt, black pepper, and drizzle with oil. Transfer the seasoned trout fillets to a cooking pan that fits the Innsky Air Fryer Oven.
3. Add green onions, ginger, orange zest, and orange juice to the cooking pan, toss well, then place in the preheated air fryer to cook for 20 minutes.
4. Divide the fish and sauce into equal portions, then serve.

Nutritional value per serving:

Calories: 239kcal, Carbs: 18g, Fat: 10g, Protein: 23g

Trout and Butter Sauce

The butter gives the trout a juicy, yummy taste. The trout will be crisp on the outside and moist on the inside.

Prep and Cooking Time: 20 minutes | Serves: 4

Ingredients To Use:

- 4 boneless trout fillets
- 2 Tbsp olive oil
- 3 Tbsp of chopped chives
- 6 Tbsp butter
- 2 tsp lemon juice
- 3 tsp of grated lemon zest
- Salt and black pepper, as desired

Step-by-Step Directions to Cook It:

1. Set the Innsky Air Fryer Oven to Fish Mode and preheat to 360°F
2. Season the trout with black pepper and salt, drizzle with oil, then transfer to the preheated air fryer.
3. Cook for 10 minutes, flipping just once at the 5 minutes mark.
4. In the meantime, heat a cooking pan placed over medium heat. Melt butter, then add salt, pepper, lemon zest and juice, and chives. Stir well, and cook for 2 minutes before removing from heat.
5. Serve butter sauce with trout fillets.

Nutritional value per serving:

Calories: 163kcal, Carbs: 14g, Fat: 6g, Protein: 8g

Creamy Salmon

The coconut cream used in this recipe transforms the taste of the salmon. Any coconut product can convert a regular meal to an exotic one.

Prep and Cooking Time: 20 minutes| Serves: 4

Ingredients To Use:

- 4 boneless salmon fillets
- 1 Tbsp extra virgin olive oil
- 1-1/2 tsp mustard
- 1/3 cup of grated cheddar cheese
- 1/2 cup of coconut cream
- 1 Tbsp of chopped parsley
- Salt and black pepper, as desired

Step-by-Step Directions to Cook It:

1. Set the Innsky Air Fryer Oven to Fish Mode and preheat to 320°F
2. Add salt and pepper to the salmon, then drizzle with oil.
3. In a separate bowl, mix the cheddar, coconut cream, salt, pepper, and mustard. Mix well.
4. Mix the salmon and coconut cream mix in a cooking pan that fits the Innsky Air Fryer Oven.
5. Transfer to the air fryer and cook for 10 minutes.
6. Divide into equal portions, garnish with parsley, and serve.

Nutritional value per serving:

Calories: 200kcal, Carbs: 17g, Fat: 6g, Protein: 20g

Salmon and Avocado Salsa

This book has so many salmon recipes because the fish simply tastes fantastic when cooked with the Innsky Air Fryer Oven.

Prep and Cooking Time: 40 minutes | Serves: 4

Ingredients To Use:

- 4 salmon fillets
- 1 tsp of garlic powder
- 1 Tbsp olive oil
- 1 tsp sweet paprika
- 1 tsp cumin, ground
- 1/2 tsp chili powder
- Salt and black pepper, as desired

Salsa Ingredients

- 1 red onion, thinly sliced
- 2 limes, juiced
- 1 avocado, peeled, pitted, and chopped
- 2 Tbsp of chopped cilantro
- Salt and black pepper, as desired

Step-by-Step Directions to Cook It:

1. Set the Innsky Air Fryer Oven to Fish Mode and preheat to 350°F
2. Mix the salt, black pepper, cumin, chili powder, paprika, onion powder, and salmon in a bowl. Toss until the salmon is well-coated. Drizzle the salmon with oil.
3. Transfer seasoned salmon to the preheated air fryer and cook each side for 5 minutes.

4. In a separate bowl, mix the avocado, salt, black pepper, red onion, cilantro, and lime juice. Stir well.
5. Divide the salmon fillets into equal portions and serve with avocado salsa.

Nutritional value per serving:

Calories: 300kcal, Carbs: 18g, Fat: 14g, Protein: 16g

Italian Barramundi Fillets and Tomato Salsa

It may be challenging to find this fish at your local grocery store, but the search is worth it. The taste of Barramundi fish fillets coated with Italian seasoning tastes is out of this world.

Prep and Cooking Time: 40 minutes | Serves: 5

Ingredients To Use:

- 2 boneless barramundi fillets, boneless
- 2 tsp Italian seasoning
- 1 Tbsp and 2 tsp of olive oil
- 1/4 cup of chopped cherry tomatoes
- 2 Tbsp of chopped parsley
- 1/4 cup of chopped black olives
- 1/4 cup green olives, pitted and chopped
- 3 Tbsp of lemon zest
- Salt and black pepper, as desired

Step-by-Step Directions to Cook It:

1. Set the Innsky Air Fryer Oven to Fish Mode and preheat to 360°F
2. Coat the fish with salt, black pepper, Italian seasoning, and 2 tsp of olive oil.
3. Transfer fish fillets to the preheated air fryer and cook for 8 minutes, flipping at halftime.
4. Meanwhile, mix the tomatoes, black olives, salt, black pepper, lemon zest and juice, green olives, 1 tablespoon of olive oil, and parsley in a separate bowl. Toss until well-combined.
5. Divide the barramundi fillets into equal portions and serve with special tomato sauce.

Nutritional value per serving:

Calories: 270kcal, Carbs: 18g, Fat: 4g, Protein: 27g

Chapter 8: Baking and Toasting Recipes

Seafood Casserole

Just a bite of this seafood combination will leave you hungry for more. Try out this recipe on your Innsky Air Fryer Oven.

Prep and Cooking Time: 50 minutes | Serves: 6

Ingredients To Use:

- 2 ounces of chopped mushrooms
- 6 Tbsp butter
- 1 celery stalk, chopped
- 1 small green bell pepper, chopped
- 1/2 cup of white wine
- 4 Tbsp flour
- 1-1/2 cups of milk
- 4 sea scallops, sliced
- 1/2 cup of heavy cream
- 4 ounces of boneless haddock, skinned and cut into portions
- 1/2 tsp of mustard powder
- 1/3 cup of bread crumbs
- 1 Tbsp lemon juice
- 2 garlic cloves, grated
- 3 Tbsp of grated cheddar cheese
- 1 tsp of sweet paprika
- A handful of chopped parsley

- 1 small yellow onion, chopped
- 4 ounces of cooked lobster meat, and cut into portions
- Salt and black pepper, as desired

Step-by-Step Directions to Cook It:

1. Set the Innsky Air Fryer Oven to Baking Mode and preheat to 360°F
2. Melt the butter in a pan placed over medium heat and add the bell pepper, mushrooms, garlic, celery, onion, and white wine— Cook for 10 minutes.
3. To the pan, add the flour, milk, and cream. Stir, and cook for 5 minutes.
4. To the same pan, add salt, pepper, lemon juice, scallops, mustard powder, haddock, and lobster meat. Stir, remove from heat and transfer the contents of the pan to a cooking pan that fits the Innsky Air Fryer Oven.
5. In a separate bowl, mix the bread crumbs, cheese, and paprika. Sprinkle the mix over the seafood combination in the cooking pan.
6. Transfer the cooking pan to the preheated air fryer and bake for 16 minutes.
7. Divide into equal portions, sprinkle with parsley, and serve.

Nutritional value per serving:

Calories: 270kcal, Carbs: 15g, Fat: 32g, Protein: 23g

Blueberry Scones

This blueberry delicacy is sure to improve your mood on sad and dull days. Try it out when you feel down

Prep and Cooking Time: 20 minutes| Serves: 10

Ingredients To Use:

- 1/2 cup heavy cream
- 1 cup of white flour
- 5 Tbsp sugar
- 1 cup of blueberries
- 1/2 cup of butter
- 2 tsp vanilla extract
- 2 medium eggs
- 2 tsp baking powder

Step-by-Step Directions to Cook It:

1. Set the Innsky Air Fryer Oven to Baking Mode and preheat to 320°F
2. Mix the flour, baking powder, salt, and blueberries in a small bowl and stir.
3. In a separate bowl, mix the butter, heavy cream, vanilla extract, eggs, and sugar. Whisk until well-combined.
4. Join the two mixtures in a large bowl and knead until the dough is formed. Create 10 triangle shapes from this mix and arrange them on a lined baking sheet proportionate to the Innsky Air Fryer Oven.
5. Transfer the baking sheet to the preheated air fryer and bake for 10 minutes.
6. Remove them from heat and allow to cool before serving.

Nutritional value per serving:

Calories: 130kcal, Carbs: 4g, Fat: 2g, Protein: 3g

Cocoa Cookies

Chocolate automatically makes everything better. Try this cookie recipe on days when you just want to let go and bake.

Prep and Cooking Time: 24 minutes | Serves: 12

Ingredients To Use:

- 6 ounces of melted coconut oil
- 2 tsp vanilla
- 6 medium eggs
- 1/2 tsp baking powder
- 3 ounces of cocoa powder
- 5 Tbsp sugar
- 4 ounces of cream cheese

Step-by-Step Directions to Cook It:

1. Set the Innsky Air Fryer Oven to Baking Mode and preheat to 320°F
2. With a mixer, blend the eggs, coconut oil, baking powder, cocoa powder, cream cheese, and vanilla.
3. Pour the blended mixture to a baking dish that is appropriate for the Innsky Air Fryer Oven.
4. Transfer the lined baking dish to the preheated air fryer—Bake for 14 minutes.
5. Cut the cookies into rectangles
6. Serve.

Nutritional value per serving:

Calories: 178 kcal, Carbs: 3g, Fat: 14g, Protein: 5g

Carrot Cake

Whoever said carrots are tasteless obviously hasn't eaten a carrot cake prepared on the Innsky Air Fryer Oven. The carrot added to the recipe gives the cake a delicious, fruity taste.

Prep and Cooking Time: 55 minutes | Serves: 6

Ingredients To Use:

- 5 ounces flour
- 3/4 tsp baking powder
- 1/3 cup of shredded coconut flakes
- 1/2 tsp of cinnamon powder
- 1/2 tsp allspice
- 3 Tbsp yogurt
- 1/4 cup of pineapple juice
- 1 medium egg
- 1/3 cup of grated carrots
- 1/2 cup of sugar
- 4 Tbsp sunflower oil
- 1/4 tsp of ground nutmeg
- 1/3 cup of chopped, toasted pecans
- 1/2 tsp baking soda
- Cooking spray
- Whipped cream, as desired.

Step-by-Step Directions to Cook It:

1. Set the Innsky Air Fryer Oven to Baking Mode and preheat to 320°F
2. Mix the flour, nutmeg, baking soda and powder, cinnamon, and allspice in a bowl.
3. In a separate bowl, mix the egg, sugar, pineapple juice, pecans, carrots, oil, and coconut flakes. Whish thoroughly.
4. Join the two mixtures in a large bowl and whisk.
5. Transfer the mixture to a greased springform pan appropriate for the Innsky Air Fryer Oven and bake for 45 minutes.
6. Allow to cool, cut the cake, top with whipped cream, and serve.

Nutritional value per serving:

Calories: 200 kcal, Carbs: 22g, Fat: 6g, Protein: 4g

Mini Lava Cakes

The juicy inside of this lava cake recipe is a treat for those who love chocolate; the lava cake simply melts in your mouth.

Prep and Cooking Time: 30 minutes | Serves: 3

Ingredients To Use:

- 1/2 tsp orange zest
- 1 large egg
- 4 Tbsp milk
- 4 Tbsp sugar
- 4 Tbsp flour
- 1 Tbsp cocoa powder
- 2 Tbsp olive oil
- 1/2 tsp baking powder
- Coconut powder, as desired.

Step-by-Step Directions to Cook It:

1. Set the Innsky Air Fryer Oven to Baking Mode and preheat to 320°F
2. Mix the egg, sugar, flour, milk, oil, cocoa powder, orange zest, and baking powder in a large bowl. Whisk thoroughly, then pour into greased ramekins.
3. Transfer the ramekins to the preheated Air Fryer Oven and bake for 20 minutes.
4. Sprinkle the cakes with coconut powder and serve warm.

Nutritional value per serving:

Calories: 201kcal, Carbs: 23g, Fat: 7g, Protein: 4g

Apple Bread

An apple a day keeps the doctors away. If you find it challenging to eat apples alone, you can try out this bread recipe that ensures you get your dose of apple.

Prep and Cooking Time: 50 minutes | Serves: 6

Ingredients To Use:

- 3 cups of cubed apples
- 1 Tbsp vanilla
- 1 cup of sugar
- 2 medium eggs
- 1 stick butter
- 2 cups white flour
- 1 Tbsp baking powder
- 1 Tbsp apple pie spice
- 1 cup of water

Step-by-Step Directions to Cook It:

1. Set the Innsky Air Fryer Oven to Baking Mode and preheat to 320°F
2. With an electric mixer, mix the egg, butter stick, sugar, and apple pie spice.
3. Add the apples to the mixture and stir.
4. In a separate bowl, mix the flour and baking powder. Stir.
5. Mix the two mixtures in a large bowl and pour it into an appropriate springform pan.
6. Transfer the pan to the preheated Air Fryer Oven and bake for 40 minutes.
7. Slice the bread and serve.

Nutritional value per serving:

Calories: 192 kcal, Carbs: 14g, Fat: 6g, Protein: 7g

Air Fried Bananas

Banana has never tasted yummier with this recipe prepared on the Innsky Air Fryer Oven. Prepare to have your mind blown with just a taste.

Prep and Cooking Time: 25 minutes | Serves: 4

Ingredients To Use:

- 3 Tbsp butter
- 1 cup panko
- 8 bananas, peeled and cut into halves
- 1/2 cup of cornflour
- 2 medium eggs, beaten
- 3 Tbsp cinnamon sugar

Step-by-Step Directions to Cook It:

1. Set the Innsky Air Fryer Oven to Baking Mode and preheat to 280°F
2. Melt the butter in a pan placed over medium heat, add the panko and stir. Cook for 4 minutes and then transfer to a small bowl.
3. Roll each of the banana halves in the flour, followed by the eggs and then the panko mix.
4. Transfer the coated bananas to the Innsky Air Fryer Oven and sprinkle with cinnamon sugar. Bake for 10 minutes.
5. Serve immediately.

Nutritional value per serving:

Calories: 164kcal, Carbs: 32g, Fat: 1g, Protein: 4g

Wrapped Pears

The pastry sheets hide the real delicacy within them. A single bite will have a combination of all the ingredients used in this recipe. What are you waiting for? Try the recipe out now.

Prep and Cooking Time: 25 minutes | Serves: 4

Ingredients To Use:

- 4 puff pastry sheets
- 2 Tbsp sugar
- 2 pears, halved
- 1 egg, whisked
- 14 ounces of vanilla custard
- 1/2 tsp cinnamon powder

Step-by-Step Directions to Cook It:

1. Set the Innsky Air Fryer Oven to Baking Mode and preheat to 320°F
2. Place the pastry slices on a flat surface, add a few spoons of vanilla custard to the center of each slice, top with the pear halves and wrap.
3. Brush each wrapped puff pastry with egg, sugar, and cinnamon.
4. Transfer the puffs to the basket of the preheated air fryer and bake for 15 minutes.
5. Serve immediately.

Nutritional value per serving:

Calories: 200 kcal, Carbs: 14g, Fat: 2g, Protein: 3g

Chapter 9: Grilling and Roasting Recipes

Roasted Pumpkin

Grilling the pumpkin leaves them dry and infused with flavor from the spices used in the preparation. Serve the meal as a side dish to a chicken meal and you wont regret it.

Prep and Cooking Time: 22 minutes | Serves: 4

Ingredients To Use:

- A pinch of cinnamon powder
- 1 Tbsp of olive oil
- A pinch of sea salt
- A pinch of brown sugar
- 3 garlic cloves, grated
- A pinch of ground nutmeg, ground
- 1-1/2 pound of pumpkin, sliced, deseeded, and chopped

Step-by-Step Directions to Cook It:

1. Preheat the Innsky Air Fryer Oven to 370°F
2. Pour pumpkin into the air fryers basket and add the garlic, oil, salt, cinnamon, brown sugar, and nutmeg. Toss well, then cover.
3. Cook in the preheated air fryer oven for 12 minutes.
4. Divide into equal portions

Nutritional value per serving:

Calories: 200kcal, Carbs: 7g, Fat: 5g, Protein: 4g

Roasted Peppers

This recipe is for people who love their pepper without a bite. Bell peppers are relatively harmless and taste delicious when eaten with a grilled meal. Serve this with grilled beef or lamb for a rich experience.

Prep and Cooking Time: 30 minutes | Serves: 4

Ingredients To Use:

- 1 Tbsp of sweet paprika
- 1 Tbsp of olive oil
- 4 red bell peppers, chopped
- 4 green bell peppers, chopped
- 4 yellow bell peppers, chopped
- 1 purple onion, chopped
- Salt and black pepper, as desired

Step-by-Step Directions to Cook It:

1. Preheat the Innsky Air Fryer Oven to 350°F
2. In the air fryer, mix the red, green, and yellow bell peppers.
3. Add the paprika to the chopped vegetable, coat with oil and add the onion, salt, and black pepper.
4. Cook for 20 minutes.
5. Divide the vegetables into 4 equal portions. serve

Nutritional value per serving:

Calories: 142kcal, Carbs: 7g, Fat: 4g, Protein: 4g

Roasted Cod and Prosciutto

The prosciutto enhances the flavor of the codfish. Your palate is seduced with the combination of two unique flavors.

Prep and Cooking Time: 20 minutes| Serves: 4

Ingredients To Use:

- 1 Tbsp of chopped parsley
- 4 medium cod fillets
- 1/4 cup of melted butter
- 2 garlic cloves, grated
- 2 Tbsp of lemon juice
- 3 Tbsp of chopped prosciutto
- 1 tsp of mustard
- 1 shallot, chopped
- Salt and black pepper, as desired

Step-by-Step Directions to Cook It:

1. Preheat the Innsky Air Fryer Oven to 390°F
2. Mix the mustard, butter, garlic, parsley, lemon juice, shallots, salt, parsley, and prosciutto. Whisk together.
3. Season the fish with salt, pepper, and prosciutto mix. Transfer the coated fish to the air fryer and cook for 10 minutes.
4. Serve.

Nutritional value per serving:

Calories: 200kcal, Carbs: 12g, Fat: 4g, Protein: 6g

Garlic Lamb Chops

Garlic is the secret weapon of most chefs. It contributes to the aroma of the food and makes meat taste better. Try this recipe out to find out the fantastic effect of garlic.

Prep and Cooking Time: 20 minutes | Serves: 4

Ingredients To Use:

- 3 Tbsp of olive oil
- 8 lamb chops
- 4 garlic cloves, grated
- 1 Tbsp of chopped oregano
- 1 Tbsp of chopped coriander
- Salt and black pepper, as desired
- Parsley sprigs to garnish (optional)

Step-by-Step Directions to Cook It:

1. Preheat the Innsky Air Fryer Oven to 400°F
2. Mix the oregano, salt, black pepper, garlic, and lamb chops in a small bowl.
3. Transfer the seasoned lamb to the Innsky rotisserie basket and cook for 5 minutes.
4. Flip the lamb and cook for another five minutes. Cut up the lamb and serve with salad.

Nutritional value per serving:

Calories: 231kcal, Carbs: 14g, Fat: 7g, Protein: 23g

Lamb Roast and Potatoes

This recipe is a full meal. The lamb and the potatoes will leave you satisfied and eager to try out new things.

Prep and Cooking Time: 3 hours 55 minutes | Serves: 6

Ingredients To Use:

- 4 pounds lamb roast
- 6 potatoes, cooked
- 4 bay leaves
- 1 spring of rosemary
- 1/2 cup lamb stock
- 3 garlic cloves, grated
- Salt and black pepper, as desired

Step-by-Step Directions to Cook It:

1. Mix all the ingredients (except cooked potatoes) in a baking dish, cover, and keep in the refrigerator for 3 hours to marinate.
2. Preheat the Innsky Air Fryer Oven to 360°F
3. Separate the lamb from the marinade and place it in the Innsky rotisserie basket.
4. Cook for 45 minutes. Flip after 25 minutes
5. Slice lamb into 6 portions and serve with cooked potatoes.

Nutritional value per serving:

Calories: 273kcal, Carbs: 25g, Fat: 4g, Protein: 29g

Beef Roast and Wine Sauce

Who doesn't love a good beef served with wine sauce? Every bite of this meal comes with an explosion of taste.

Prep and Cooking Time: 1 hour 35 minutes | Serves: 6

Ingredients To Use:

- 3 pounds of beef roast
- 17 ounces beef stock
- 3 ounces of red wine
- 1/2 tsp of chicken salt
- 1/2 tsp of smoked paprika
- 1 yellow onion, chopped
- 4 garlic cloves, minced
- 3 carrots, chopped
- 5 potatoes, chopped
- Salt and black pepper, as desired

Step-by-Step Directions to Cook It:

1. Preheat the Innsky Air Fryer Oven to 360°F
2. Mix the salt, pepper, paprika, and chicken salt in a bowl, rub the seasoning mix on the beef.
3. Transfer the beef to the Innsky Air Fryer Oven basket and cook 45 minutes. Flip after 45 minutes.
4. Remove the lamb from the air fryer.
5. Mix the rest of the ingredients in a cooking pan that can fit your air fryer and cook for another 30 minutes at the same temperature.
6. Cut the lamb into slice and serve with the cooked potatoes mix.

Nutritional value per serving:

Calories: 304kcal, Carbs: 20g, Fat: 20g, Protein: 32g

Short Ribs and Beer Sauce

With this recipe, you don't need to drink a bottle of beer to get that lovely alcoholic taste. Every bite of the lamb and potato is infused with flavor from the beer sauce.

Prep and Cooking Time: 60 minutes| Serves: 6

Ingredients To Use:

- 5 4 pounds short ribs, cut into small pieces
- 1 yellow onion, chopped
- Salt and black pepper to the taste
- 1/4 cup tomato paste
- 1 cup dark beer
- 1 cup chicken stock
- 1 bay leaf
- 6 thyme springs, chopped
- 1 Portobello mushroom, dried

Step-by-Step Directions to Cook It:

1. Preheat the Innsky Air Fryer Oven to 350°F
2. To prepare the sauce, heat the tomato paste, beer, mushroom, bay leaves, onions, salt, black pepper, and thyme in a pan placed over medium heat. Cook for 10 minutes and then set aside.
3. Season lamb with salt, pepper, and thyme. Transfer to the Innsky air fryer basket and grill for 30 minutes. Flip after 20 minutes.
4. Cut up the lamb and serve with the beer sauce.

Nutritional value per serving:

Calories: 300kcal, Carbs: 18g, Fat: 7g, Protein: 23g

Beef patties for Burgers and Sandwiches.

With the Innsky Air Power Oven, you don't have to drag out your grill before you make a burger. Try out this recipe when you are in the mood for burgers.

Prep and Cooking Time: 25 minutes| Serves: 6

Ingredients To Use:

- 2 pounds of ground beef
- Salt and black pepper, as desired
- 1/2 tsp garlic powder
- 1 Tbsp soy sauce
- 1/4 cup beef stock
- 3/4 cup flour
- 1 Tbsp of chopped parsley
- 1 Tbsp onion flakes

Step-by-Step Directions to Cook It:

1. Preheat the Innsky Air Fryer Oven to 350°F
2. in a medium bowl, mix the beef with salt, black pepper, garlic, soy sauce, beef stock, parsley, flour, and onion flakes. Toss until well-combined
3. Form about six patties with the flour dough and place them in the Innsky Air Fryer. Grill for 7 minutes per side.
4. Serve beef patties with buns or bread.

Nutritional value per serving:

Calories: 435kcal, Carbs: 6g, Fat: 23g, Protein: 32g

Chapter 10: Rotisserie Recipes

Herbed Chicken

The aroma and flavor from the herbs and the fact that a whole chicken is used in this recipe will put you in a festive mood.

Prep and Cooking Time: 1 hour 10 minutes| Serves: 4

Ingredients To Use:

- 1 whole chicken
- 1 tsp garlic powder
- 1/2 tsp thyme, dried
- 1 Tbsp lemon juice
- 1 tsp rosemary, dried
- 1 tsp onion powder
- 2 Tbsp olive oil
- Salt and black pepper, as desired

Step-by-Step Directions to Cook It:

1. Set the Innsky Air Fryer Oven to Rotisserie Mode and preheat to 360°F
2. Season the whole chicken with salt, black pepper, thyme, garlic, rosemary, onion, lemon juice, and oil. Leave to marinate for 30 minutes.
3. Transfer the marinated chicken to the Innsky Air Fryer Oven's Rotisserie Basket and turn on the rotating button. Cook for 20 minutes.
4. Remove whole chicken from the air fryer and allow it to cool before carving and serving.

Nutritional value per serving:

Calories: 390kcal, Carbs: 22g, Fat: 10g, Protein: 20g

Chinese Stuffed Chicken

This whole chicken recipe will remind you of Thanksgiving. From the stuffing to the aroma, everything just contributes to a festive feeling. Share the meal with your neighbors and celebrate with your delightful Innsky Air Fryer Oven.

Prep and Cooking Time: 45 minutes | Serves: 8

Ingredients To Use:

- 1 whole chicken
- 2 red chilies, chopped
- 10 wolfberries
- 4 ginger slices
- 1 tsp soy sauce
- 1 yam, diced
- 3 tsp sesame oil
- Salt and white pepper, as desired

Step-by-Step Directions to Cook It:

1. Set the Innsky Air Fryer Oven to Rotisserie Mode and preheat to 400°F
2. Season the whole chicken with salt, black pepper, soy sauce, and sesame oil, then stuff it with wolfberries, diced yam, chilies, and ginger.
3. Transfer the chicken to the preheated Innsky Air Fryer Oven's Rotisserie Basket and turn on the Rotating Button. Cook for 20 minutes. After this, reduce the temperature to 360°F and cook for another 15 minutes.
4. Cut the chicken into pieces, then serve.

Nutritional value per serving:

Calories: 320kcal, Carbs: 22g, Fat: 12g, Protein: 12

Rotisserie Duck and Veggies

Prepare a restaurant-worthy duck with the rotisserie cooking option available in the Innsky Air Fryer Oven.

Prep and Cooking Time: 40 minutes| Serves: 8

Ingredients To Use:

- 1 whole duck
- 3 cucumbers, sliced into rounds
- 2 carrots, diced
- 1 small ginger piece, minced
- Salt and black pepper, as desired

Step-by-Step Directions to Cook It:

1. Set the Innsky Air Fryer Oven to Rotisserie Mode and preheat to 400°F
2. Season duck with salt, black pepper, and ginger. Transfer whole duck to the rotisserie basket and cook for 30 minutes. Make sure to turn on the rotation button.
3. Carve the duck and serve with cucumber rounds and carrots.

Nutritional value per serving:

Calories: 200kcal, Carbs: 20g, Fat: 10g, Protein: 22g

Rotisserie Chicken and Apricot Sauce

The taste of apricot on the skin of the chicken transforms everyone's definition of a tasty chicken. This chicken meal is out of this world.

Prep and Cooking Time: 50 minutes | Serves: 4

Ingredients To Use:

- 1 whole chicken
- 1 Tbsp olive oil
- 2 Tbsp honey
- 1/2 tsp of smoked paprika
- 1/4 cup of apricot preserves
- 1/4 cup of white wine
- 1/2 tsp of dried marjoram
- 2 Tbsp of white vinegar
- 1/4 cup of chicken stock
- 1-1/2 tsp ginger, grated
- Salt and black pepper, as desired

Step-by-Step Directions to Cook It:

1. Set the Innsky Air Fryer Oven to Rotisserie Mode and preheat to 360°F
2. Season the whole chicken with salt, black pepper, marjoram, paprika, and oil.
3. Transfer the coated chicken to the rotisserie basket, set the timer for 30 minutes, and turn on the rotating button.
4. Mix all the other ingredients (with salt) in a cooking pan that fits the Innsky Air Fryer Oven. Transfer the apricot sauce to the oven once the chicken is done and cook for 10 minutes.
5. Carve the chicken and serve with apricot sauce.

Nutritional value per serving:

Calories: 200kcal, Carbs: 20g, Fat: 7g, Protein: 14g

Provencal Pork

The combination of pork and herbs will always result in a lovely meal.

Prep and Cooking Time: 30 minutes | Serves: 2

Ingredients To Use:

- 1 red onion, sliced
- 1 yellow bell pepper, cut into strips
- 1 green bell pepper, cut into strips
- Salt and black pepper to the taste
- 2 tsp Provencal herbs
- 1/2 Tbsp mustard
- 1 Tbsp olive oil
- 7 ounces pork tenderloin

Step-by-Step Directions to Cook It:

1. Set the Innsky Air Fryer Oven to Rotisserie Mode and preheat to 370°F
2. Mix all the bell peppers, onion, salt, black pepper, Provencal herbs, and 1/2 Tbsp of oil in a small bowl.
3. Season pork with salt, pepper, and mustard. Transfer to the rotisserie basket and place it in the preheated air fryer—Cook for 15 minutes.
4. Transfer veggies to a baking dish and place it in the air fryer—Cook for 8 minutes.
5. Slice the pork into proportionate pieces and serve with veggies.

Nutritional value per serving:

Calories: 300kcal, Carbs: 21g, Fat: 7g, Protein: 23g

Crispy Lamb

Macadamia nuts and lamb is a lovely combination. It is healthy and filling.

Prep and Cooking Time: 40 minutes | Serves: 4

Ingredients To Use:

- 1 Tbsp bread crumbs
- 1 Tbsp olive oil
- 1 garlic clove, minced
- 1 egg
- 28 ounces rack of lamb
- 1 Tbsp of chopped rosemary
- 2 Tbsp macadamia nuts, toasted and crushed
- Salt and black pepper, as desired

Step-by-Step Directions to Cook It:

1. Set the Innsky Air Fryer Oven to Rotisserie Mode and preheat to 360°F
2. Prepare a rub by mixing oil and garlic.
3. Season the lamb with salt and pepper, coat with the rub, and set aside.
4. In a bowl, mix the nuts, breadcrumbs, and rosemary.
5. In a separate bowl, whisk the eggs.
6. Dip the seasoned lamb in the egg, then coat it with the macadamia and finally transfer it to the Innsky Air Fryer Oven's rotisserie basket. Turn on the rotation button and cook for 25 minutes.
7. Increase the temperature to 400°F and cook for an additional 5 minutes.
8. Divide into 4 equal portions and serve.

Nutritional value per serving:

Calories: 230kcal, Carbs: 10g, Fat: 2g, Protein: 12g

Marinated Pork Chops and Onions

After 24 hours of marinating, the pork in this recipe lives and breates flavor. The onions are a nice addition.

Prep and Cooking Time: 24 hours 25 minutes| Serves: 6

Ingredients To Use:

- 2 pork chops
- 2 yellow onions, sliced
- 1/4 cup olive oil
- 2 garlic cloves, minced
- 1 tsp sweet paprika
- 2 tsp mustard
- 1/2 tsp oregano, dried
- A pinch of cayenne pepper
- 1/2 tsp of dried thyme
- Salt and black pepper, as desired

Step-by-Step Directions to Cook It:

1. Mix the oil, garlic, mustard, black pepper, paprika, cayenne, and thyme in a small bowl. Combine well.
2. Add the meat to the mustard mix, cover, and keep in the refrigerator for 24 hours.
3. Set the Innsky Air Fryer Oven to Rotisserie Mode and preheat to 360°F
4. Transfer meat and onions to the rotisserie basket and cook for 25 minutes, while rotating.
5. Cut meat into portions and serve.

Nutritional value per serving:

Calories: 384kcal, Carbs: 17g, Fat: 4g, Protein: 25g

Cod Fillets and Pea

The peas are chewy, and when combined with the fish, it gives a small burst of flavor.

Prep and Cooking Time: 20 minutes| Serves: 4

Ingredients To Use:

- 4 boneless cod fillets
- 2 cups of peas
- 4 Tbsp of wine
- 2 Tbsp of chopped parsley
- 1/2 tsp of sweet paprika
- 2 garlic cloves, grated
- 1/2 tsp of dried oregano
- Salt and pepper, as desired

Step-by-Step Directions to Cook It:

1. Set the Innsky Air Fryer Oven to Rotisserie Mode and preheat to 360°F
2. Blend the parsley, black pepper, paprika, oregano, and wine in a food processor to obtain a smooth mixture.
3. Coat the cod fillets with the blended mix, transfer to rotisserie basket, and cook for 10 minutes. Make sure to turn on the rotating button.
4. In a separate pot placed over medium heat, bring the water to a boil and cook the peas for 10 minutes.
5. Drain the cooked peas and divide into equal portions. Serve with rotisserie fish pieces.

Nutritional value per serving:

Calories: 261kcal, Carbs: 20g, Fat: 8g, Protein: 22g

Chapter 11: Vegetarian Recipes

Balsamic Artichokes

Each leaf of the artichoke has been infused with the delicious flavor of the spices used during the preparation. Try to discover the taste.

Prep and Cooking Time: 17 minutes | Serves: 4

Ingredients To Use:

- 4 artichokes, trimmed
- 2 Tbsp lemon juice
- 2 tsp of balsamic vinegar
- 2 garlic cloves, grated
- 1 tsp of dried oregano
- Salt and black pepper, as desired
- 1/4 cup of extra virgin olive oil

Step-by-Step Directions to Cook It:

1. Preheat the Innsky Air Fryer Oven to 360°F
2. Season the artichokes with salt, black pepper, 1/8 cup of olive oil, and 1 tablespoon of lemon juice.
3. Transfer coated artichokes to preheated air fryer and cook for 7 minutes.
4. While artichokes are cooking, mix the remaining lemon juice, oil, salt, black pepper, vinegar, oregano, and garlic. Combine well.
5. Arrange the artichokes on a plate and drizzle with the prepared balsamic vinaigrette.
6. Serve.

Nutritional value per serving:

Calories: 200kcal, Carbs: 12g, Fat: 3g, Protein: 4g

Beets and Arugula Salad

The beets are more comfortable to chew after they are roasted. Also, the heat from the Innsky Air Fryer Oven makes the flavor stick.

Prep and Cooking Time: 20 minutes | Serves: 4

Ingredients To Use:

- 1-1/2 pound of beet, peeled cut into quarters
- 2 tsp grated orange zest
- 2 Tbsp of brown sugar
- 1 tsp of olive oil
- 1/4 cup of walnut
- 2 Tbsp of cider vinegar
- 1/2 cup of orange juice
- 2 scallions, sliced
- 2 cups of arugula
- 2 tsp of Goat cheese

Step-by-Step Directions to Cook It:

1. Preheat the Innsky Air Fryer Oven to 350°F
2. Coat the beets with oil and orange juice.
3. Transfer the coated beats to the preheated air fryer and cook for 20 minutes.
4. Mix the prepared beets, arugula, orange zest, walnuts, and scallions in a bowl. Toss well
5. In another bowl, mix the sugar, vinegar, and goat cheese. Toss until well-combined.
6. Divide the beets mixture into equal portions and serve with cheese mix
7. Serve.

Nutritional value per serving:

Calories: 121 kcal, Carbs: 11 g, Fat: 2g, Protein: 4g

Broccoli Salad

It is easier to eat your vegetables when they are seasoned to perfection. Try this broccoli recipe to understand the real meaning of seasoning.

Prep and Cooking Time: 18 minutes | Serves: 4

Ingredients To Use:

- 1 Tbsp of peanut oil
- 1 head of broccoli with the florets separated
- 1 Tbsp Chinese rice wine vinegar
- 6 garlic cloves, grated
- Salt and black pepper, as desired

Step-by-Step Directions to Cook It:

1. Preheat the Innsky Air Fryer Oven to 350°F
2. Mix the broccoli, salt, pepper, and ½ tablespoon of peanut oil in a bowl.
3. Transfer the coated broccoli to the preheated air fryer's basket and cook for 8 minutes. Shake the basket after 4 minutes.
4. Remove the broccoli from the air fryer and mix with the leftover peanut oil, rice vinegar, and garlic. Toss well.
5. Serve.

Nutritional value per serving:

Calories: 121 kcal, Carbs: 4g, Fat: 3g, Protein: 4g

Brussel Sprouts and Tomato Mix

Tomatoes are juicy and sweet. When combined with Brussels, they overpower the taste of the vegetable and make it easier to chew.

Prep and Cooking Time: 15 minutes | Serves: 4

Ingredients To Use:

- 1 pound of Brussels sprouts, trimmed
- 1/4 cup of chopped green onions
- 6 cherry tomatoes, cut into halves
- 1 Tbsp olive oil
- Salt and black pepper, as desired

Step-by-Step Directions to Cook It:

1. Preheat the Innsky Air Fryer Oven to 350°F
2. Season Brussels with salt and black pepper, add them to the preheated air fryer, and cook for 10 minutes.
3. Transfer the cooked Brussels to a bowl and mix with salt, black pepper, tomatoes, green onions, and oil. Toss until well combined.
4. Serve.

Nutritional value per serving:

Calories: 121kcal, Carbs: 114g, Fat: 4g, Protein: 4g

Spicy Cabbage

This is for those who love their pepper with a kick. The red pepper flakes completely transform the cabbage.

Prep and Cooking Time: 18 minutes | Serves: 4

Ingredients To Use:

- 1 carrot, grated
- 1 cabbage, chopped into fat slices
- 1/2 tsp cayenne pepper
- 1 Tbsp of sesame seed oil
- 1/4 cups of apple juice
- 1/4 cup of apple cider vinegar
- 1 tsp of crushed red pepper flakes

Step-by-Step Directions to Cook It:

1. Preheat the Innsky Air Fryer Oven to 350°F
2. In a cooking pan appropriate for your air fryer, mix the cabbage, oil, vinegar, carrot, pepper flakes, cayenne, and apple juice. Toss until well-combined.
3. Transfer to the preheated air fryer and cook for 8 minutes.
4. Divide the cabbage mix into equal portions and serve.

Nutritional value per serving:

Calories: 100 kcal, Carbs: 11 g, Fat: 4g, Protein: 7g

Beets and Blue Cheese Salad

The combination of beet and cheese will result in a burst of flavor that cannot be described with mere words. Try this recipe out to understand better.

Prep and Cooking Time: 24 minutes | Serves: 6

Ingredients To Use:

- 6 beets, peeled and cut into quarters
- 1 Tbsp olive oil
- 1/4 cup of crumbled blue cheese
- Salt and black pepper, as desired

Step-by-Step Directions to Cook It:

1. Preheat the Innsky Air Fryer Oven to 350°F
2. Add beets to the preheated air fryer and cook for 14 minutes.
3. Mix the cooked beets with blue cheese, salt, black pepper, and oil. Toss until the beet is well-coated.
4. Serve.

Nutritional value per serving:

Calories: 100kcal, Carbs: 10g, Fat: 4g, Protein: 5g

Air Fried Leeks

Fry your leeks with just one tablespoon of butter. This is only possible with the Innsky Air Fryer Oven.

Prep and Cooking Time: 17 minutes | Serves: 4

Ingredients To Use:

- 4 leeks, rinsed, ends trimmed and halved
- 1 Tbsp of melted butter
- 1 Tbsp of lemon juice
- Salt and black pepper, as desired

Step-by-Step Directions to Cook It:

1. Preheat the Innsky Air Fryer Oven to 350°F
2. Coat the leeks with melted butter, salt, and black pepper.
3. Transfer coated leeks to the preheated air fryer and cook for 7 minutes.
4. Arrange the prepared leeks on a platter, drizzle with lemon juice, and serve.

Nutritional value per serving:

Calories: 100 kcal, Carbs: 6g, Fat: 4g, Protein: 2g

Brussel Sprouts and Butter Sauce

Butter adds a much-needed creamy taste to the Brussels. Try this recipe out; it results in a delectable meal.

Prep and Cooking Time: 14 minutes | Serves: 4

Ingredients To Use:

- 1 pound of Brussels sprouts, trimmed
- 1 Tbsp butter
- 1/2 cup cooked, chopped bacon
- 2 Tbsp dill, finely chopped
- 1 Tbsp mustard
- Salt and black pepper, as desired

Step-by-Step Directions to Cook It:

1. Preheat the Innsky Air Fryer Oven to 350°F
2. Add the brussels sprouts to the preheated air fryer and cook for 10 minutes.
3. Melt the butter in a pan placed over medium heat, add the mustard, bacon, and dill. Whisk well.
4. Divide the Brussels into equal portions, then drizzle the melted butter sauce all over the vegetable.
5. Serve.

Nutritional value per serving:

Calories: 162kcal, Carbs: 14g, Fat: 8g, Protein: 5g

Chapter 12: Snacks and Desserts

Peach Pie

Try out this peach pie recipe when you are in a celebratory mood. It will heighten your feeling of joy—all good foods do.

Prep and Cooking Time: 45 minutes | Serves: 4

Ingredients To Use:

- 1 pie dough
- 2-1/4 pounds of chopped peaches
- 2 Tbsp of cornstarch
- 1/2 cup of sugar
- 2 Tbsp of flour
- A pinch of ground nutmeg
- 1 Tbsp of dark rum
- 1 Tbsp of lemon juice
- 2 Tbsp of melted butter

Step-by-Step Directions to Cook It:

1. Set the Innsky Air Fryer Oven to Baking Mode and preheat to 350°F
2. Prepare a pie pan that fits the Innsky Air Fryer Oven, roll the pie dough into the pan, and press well.
3. Mix the peaches, sugar, cornstarch, flour, nutmeg, lemon juice, rum, and butter in a bowl. Stir until well-combined.
4. Pour the peach mixture into the pie pan, then transfer the pan to the Innsky Air Fryer Oven and cook for 35 minutes.
5. Serve after allowing to cool

Nutritional value per serving:

Calories: 231kcal, Carbs: 9g, Fat: 6g, Protein: 5g

Sweet Potato Cheesecake

Now here is a cake recipe that resembles a slice of heaven. Make the cheesecake for the week and serve as a dessert.

Prep and Cooking Time: 15 minutes | Serves: 4

Ingredients To Use:

- 6 ounces 0f soft mascarpone
- 4 Tbsp of melted butter
- 8 ounces of soft cream cheese, soft
- 3/4 cup of milk
- 2/3 cup of sweet potato puree
- 1 tsp vanilla extract
- 1/4 tsp of cinnamon powder
- 2/3 cup of crumbled graham crackers

Step-by-Step Directions to Cook It:

1. Mix the butter and crackers in a bowl. Stir well and press the mixture to the bottom of a cake pan that is appropriate for the Innsky Air Fryer Oven. Set the pan aside and keep in the refrigerator.
2. In a separate bowl, mix the mascarpone, cream cheese, potato puree, cinnamon, milk, and vanilla. Whisk until well-combined.
3. Spread the potato mixture over the crust in the refrigerated cake pan.
4. Transfer the cake pan to the preheated Innsky Air Fryer Oven at 300°F. Cook for 4 minutes before transferring the contents of the cake pan to the refrigerator.
5. Allow to spend a few hours in the refrigerator before serving.

Nutritional value per serving:

Calories: 172 kcal, Carbs: 8g, Fat: 8g, Protein: 3g

Plum Bars

The bars are more delicious than they look. You simply have to try it out to know.

Prep and Cooking Time: 26 minutes | Serves: 8

Ingredients To Use:

- 2 cups of dried plums
- 2 Tbsp of melted butter
- 6 Tbsp water
- 2 cups of rolled oats
- 1 tsp cinnamon powder
- 1/2 tsp baking soda
- 1 egg, beaten
- 1 cup of brown sugar
- Cooking spray

Step-by-Step Directions to Cook It:

1. Set the Innsky Air Fryer Oven to Baking Mode and preheat to 350°F
2. Add the plums and water to a food processor. Pulse until you obtain a sticky spread.
3. In a bowl, mix the oats, baking soda, cinnamon, egg, sugar, and butter. Whisk until well-combined.
4. Divide the oat mix into two equal portions and add half of it to a baking pan that is appropriate for the Innsky Air Fryer Oven. Add cooking oil, spread the entire plum mix to the pan, then top with the leftover oat mix.
5. Transfer the baking pan to the preheated air-fryer—Cook for 16 minutes.
6. Allow to cool before cutting into medium bars and serving.

Nutritional value per serving:

Calories: 111kcal, Carbs: 12g, Fat: 5g, Protein: 6g

Pears and Espresso Cream

Everything tastes good with whipped cream; the pear in this recipe is not an exception.

Prep and Cooking Time: 40 minutes | Serves: 4

Ingredients To Use:

- 2 Tbsp lemon juice
- 4 pears, cored and cut into halves
- 2 Tbsp water
- 1 Tbsp sugar
- 2 Tbsp butter

Cream Ingredients

- 1/3 cup of sugar
- 1 cup of mascarpone
- 2 Tbsp of cold espresso
- 1 cup of whipped cream

Step-by-Step Directions to Cook It:

1. Set the Innsky Air Fryer Oven to Baking Mode and preheat to 360°F
2. Mix the halved pears, lemon juice, butter, 1 tablespoon of sugar, and water in a bowl. Mix thoroughly, then transfer to the preheated air fryer and cook for 30 minutes.
3. While cooking, prepare the cream by mixing the mascarpone, whipped cream, leftover sugar, and espresso in a bowl. Whisk until well-combined, then keep in the refrigerator.
4. When pears are done cooking, divide them into equal portions and serve with refrigerated espresso cream.

Nutritional value per serving:

Calories: 211kcal, Carbs: 8g, Fat: 5g, Protein: 7g

Air Fried Stuffed Apples

Due to its numerous health benefits, there are a lot of creative methods available to transform the taste of apple from regular to extraordinary. This recipe is one of those methods.

Prep and Cooking Time: 27 minutes | Serves: 4

Ingredients To Use:

- 4 medium apples, cored
- A handful of raisins
- 1 Tbsp of ground cinnamon
- Raw honey, as desired

Step-by-Step Directions to Cook It:

1. Preheat the Innsky Air Fryer Oven to 367°F
2. Fill up each cored apple with raisins, a sprinkle of cinnamon, and a drizzle of honey.
3. Transfer stuffed apple to the preheated air fryer and cook for 17 minutes.
4. Allow to cool before serving.

Nutritional value per serving:

Calories: 220kcal, Carbs: 6g, Fat: 3g, Protein: 10g

Berries Mix

It can't get better than the mixture of strawberries and blueberries; the combination of two or more berries is always marvelous.

Prep and Cooking Time: 11 minutes | Serves: 4

Ingredients To Use:

- 1/4 cup of torn basil leaves
- 2 Tbsp lemon juice
- 1-1/2 Tbsp champagne vinegar
- 1 Tbsp olive oil
- 1-1/2 Tbsp maple syrup
- 1 pound of halved strawberries
- 1-1/2 cups of blueberries

Step-by-Step Directions to Cook It:

1. Preheat the Innsky Air Fryer Oven to 310°F
2. In a cooking pan that is appropriate for your Innsky Air Fryer Oven, mix the maple syrup, lemon juice, and vinegar. Place the pan over medium heat and bring to a boil.
3. Add the blueberries and strawberries to the pan, then transfer to the preheated air fryer—Cook for 7 minutes.
4. Sprinkle basil over the top and serve.

Nutritional value per serving:

Calories: 163kcal, Carbs: 10g, Fat: 4g, Protein: 2.1g

Blueberry Pudding

A slice of this is sure to change your day for the better. Relive your stress by eating this at the end of the day; blueberries are known to be good for stress.

Prep and Cooking Time: 35 minutes| Serves: 6

Ingredients To Use:

- 2 cups of flour
- 3 Tbsp maple syrup
- 2 cups of rolled oats
- 1 cup of chopped walnuts
- 8 cups of blueberries
- 1 stick of melted butter
- 2 Tbsp of chopped rosemary

Step-by-Step Directions to Cook It:

1. Set the Innsky Air Fryer Oven to Baking Mode and preheat to 350°F
2. Grease a baking pan appropriate for the Innsky Air Fryer Oven and then spread the blueberries in them. Set aside.
3. Add the rolled oats, flour, butter, walnuts, rosemary and maple syrup to a food processor. Pulse until well-blended.
4. Pour the oats spread over the blueberries in the baking pan, then transfer the pan to the preheated air fryer—Cook for 25 minutes.
5. Allow to cool before cutting and serving.

Nutritional value per serving:

Calories: 150kcal, Carbs: 7g, Fat: 3, Protein: 4g

Macaroons

This is a low-calorie snack that can be eaten at any time of the day. Prepare them and take them along with you to work; it will take the edge off.

Prep and Cooking Time: 18 minutes| Serves: 20

Ingredients To Use:

- 1 tsp vanilla extract
- 4 egg whites
- 2 cups of shredded coconut
- 2 Tbsp sugar

Step-by-Step Directions to Cook It:

1. Set the Innsky Air Fryer Oven to Baking Mode and preheat to 340°F
2. Mix the egg whites and stevia with an electric mixer.
3. Add the shredded coconut and a tsp of vanilla extract to the egg mix, whisk again. You will be able to shape small balls from the whisked mixture. Add the balls to the preheated air fryer and cook for 8 minutes.
4. Serve the air fried macaroons cold.

Nutritional value per serving:

Calories: 55kcal, Carbs: 2g, Fat: 6g, Protein: 1g

Conclusion

Your family meal just got tastier and healthier with the Innsky Air-Fryer Oven doing your cooking. Power on your appliance and keep cooking these delicious and easy recipes.

Good luck!

Measurement Conversion Chart

Metric to standard	Fahrenheit to Celsius	Cups to Tbsp	Oz to grams
5 ml = 1 tsp 15 ml = 1 tbsp 30 ml = 1 fluid oz 240 ml = 1 cup 1 liter = 34 fluid oz 1 liter = 4.2 cups 1 grams = 0.035 oz 100 grams = 3.5 oz 500 grams = 1.10 lb	180 F = 80 C 270 F = 130 C 300 F = 150 C 330 F = 165 C 350 F = 180 C 400 F = 200 C	3 tsp = 1 tbsp 1/8 cup of = 2 tbsp 1/4 cup of = 4 tbsp 1/3 cup of = 5 tbsp + 1 tsp 1/2 cup of = 8 tbsp 3/4 cup of = 12 tbsp 1 cup of = 16 tbsp 8 fluid oz = 1 cup of 1 pint 2 cups = 16 fluid oz 1 quart 2 pints = 4 cups 1 gallon 4 quarts = 16 cups	1 oz = 29 g 2 oz = 57 g 3 oz = 85 g 4 oz = 113 g 5 oz = 142 g 6 oz = 170 g 7 oz = 198 g 8 oz = 227 g 10 oz = 283 g 20 oz = 567 g 30 oz = 850 g 40 oz = 1133 g

Manufactured by Amazon.ca
Bolton, ON

27427559R00061